MW01285655

UN LIMITED

STUDY GUIDE

BENNY TATE

WITH STACEY HENSLEY

Ps. 37:25

CHARISMA
HOUSE

UNLIMITED STUDY GUIDE by Benny Tate
Published by Charisma House, an imprint of Charisma Media
1150 Greenwood Blvd., Lake Mary, Florida 32746

Copyright © 2024 by Benny Tate. All rights reserved.

Unless otherwise noted, all Scripture quotations are taken from The ESV® Bible (The Holy Bible, English Standard Version®), copyright © 2001 by Crossway, a publishing ministry of Good News Publishers. Used by permission. All rights reserved.

Scripture quotations marked KJV are from the King James Version of the Bible.

Scripture quotations marked NASB are taken from the (NASB®) New American Standard Bible®, Copyright © 1960, 1971, 1977, 1995 by The Lockman Foundation. Used by permission. All rights reserved. www.lockman.org

Scripture quotations marked NKJV are taken from the New King James Version®. Copyright © 1982 by Thomas Nelson. Used by permission. All rights reserved.

Scripture quotations marked NLT are taken from the Holy Bible, New Living Translation, copyright ©1996, 2004, 2015 by Tyndale House Foundation. Used by permission of Tyndale House Publishers, Carol Stream, Illinois 60188. All rights reserved.

While the author has made every effort to provide accurate, up-to-date source information at the time of publication, statistics and other data are constantly updated. Neither the publisher nor the author assumes any responsibility for errors or for changes that occur after publication. Further, the publisher and author do not have any control over and do not assume any responsibility for third-party websites or their content.

For more resources like this, visit MyCharismaShop.com and the author's website at pastorbennytate.com.

Cataloging-in-Publication Data is on file with the Library of Congress.
International Standard Book Number: 978-1-63641-408-9

01 2024
Printed in India

Most Charisma Media products are available at special quantity discounts for bulk purchase for sales promotions, premiums, fund-raising, and educational needs. For details, call us at (407) 333-0600 or visit our website at www.charismamedia.com.

CONTENTS

WEEK FOUR: RE**S**T: STUDY SCRIPTURE AND PRAY

WEEK FIVE: RES**T**: TRUST THE HOLY SPIRIT

WEEK SIX: BENEFITS OF THE HOLY SPIRIT

INTRODUCTION

It is the Spirit who gives life; the flesh is no help at all. The words that I [Jesus] have spoken to you are spirit and life.

—JOHN 6:63

I AM SO HUMBLED that you chose to pick up this study guide and join me in learning more about the unlimited power of the Holy Spirit. I want big things for you—and so does God! I have experienced the power of the Holy Spirit in my life, and my prayer is that you will know His power too. What God has done in my life is "unlimited," but that's not because I'm so special. We all matter so much to God that He put His Spirit inside each of us. When I think that God put His Spirit in someone like me, I can't help but tell others they can experience the same thing. I want to see the church at large unified, glorifying God, and living in the fullness of the Holy Spirit.

Bible teacher Warren Wiersbe said this: "The church was born when the Spirit of God descended on the Day of Pentecost (Acts 2), and its life comes from the Spirit. When the Spirit is grieved, the church begins to lose life and power. When sin is confessed and church members get right with God and with each other, then the Spirit infuses new life—revival!"[1]

The greatest decision anyone can make is the decision to give his or her life to Jesus Christ. When we make that choice, we are given the Holy Spirit—and that means we have unlimited access to everything God has for us. The church does not talk about the Holy Spirit much, and many Christians are missing out on God's biggest blessings because they do not understand this treasure we are given the moment we receive Jesus.

Not teaching more on the Holy Spirit is one of my deepest regrets as a pastor. A few years ago I decided to remedy this, and there has been a change at our church ever since. I want this kind of change for every church and every follower of Jesus Christ. What God will do when we allow Him access and understand His power is unlimited.

The Book of Acts is full of examples of how the power of the Holy Spirit impacts the church. Throughout Luke's account of the early church we see these three outcomes repeatedly:

1. The church was unified.

2. The church was magnified.

3. The church multiplied.

Beyond seeing people come to Christ, my greatest pastoral desire is that the church be unified, magnified, and multiplied so God's glory will be on full display for a lost and hurting world. If the church exhibited these characteristics, I believe we would see a great shift in our world.

My prayer is that this study will help you better understand the character of the Holy Spirit and give you tangible ways to become a clean, empty vessel ready to receive all that God intends for you. I pray that as you work through this study guide, you will come to know the Holy Spirit and experience the abundant life God has called you to. I pray this study will help you grow in your knowledge of God's Word and apply it in your everyday life. Most important, I pray that your understanding of the Holy Spirit leads you to realize God's deep love for you so you can heal from past hurt, see the power of the Holy Spirit fully activated in your life, and draw others to Jesus as they encounter His power working in and through you.

WHAT IS THIS STUDY GUIDE ABOUT?

As you may have guessed, this study guide is all about the Holy Spirit. I want to make sure everyone understands who the Holy Spirit is, how to access His power in their lives, and the benefits of knowing Him. God established the church to glorify Jesus and do His work, and that can only be accomplished through the unlimited power of the Holy Spirit.

WHY IS STUDYING THE HOLY SPIRIT IMPORTANT?

Studying the Holy Spirit is important because the Holy Spirit is *Jesus living inside of us*. If we have invited Jesus into our lives as Lord and Savior, then we have access to the same power He had while He walked on earth. The Holy Spirit is the least talked about aspect of God in our churches today, and by not acknowledging the power of the Holy Spirit, we neglect living in the unlimited power God has for us. Some of us live with fire insurance when we have power to call down fire from heaven! Jesus came and died so we could live abundant lives, but too many of us are barely living. The Holy Spirit can change our lives if we allow Him full access, but most of us don't know how. Like the psalmist, may your prayer be, "Open my eyes, that I may behold wondrous things out of your law" (Ps. 119:18).

WHO IS THIS STUDY FOR?

Romans 8:14 tells us that "*all* who are led by the Spirit of God are sons of God" (emphasis added). This study guide is for *everybody*!

I like to pay special attention to the first time something is mentioned in Scripture. This is especially true when it comes to the Holy Spirit. Although we read about the Holy Spirit being poured out on the church in the Book of Acts, the first time the Lord filled someone with His Spirit was way back in the Book of Exodus:

> See, I have called by name Bezalel the son of Uri, the son of Hur, of the tribe of Judah. And I have *filled him with the Spirit of God*, in wisdom, in understanding, in knowledge, and in all manner of workmanship, to design artistic works, to work in gold, in silver, in bronze, in cutting jewels for setting, in carving wood, and to work in all manner of workmanship.
> —Exodus 31:2–5, NKJV, EMPHASIS ADDED

God filled Bezalel, a craftsman, with His Spirit. He did not choose a priest or a Torah scholar. He did not even say Bezalel was perfect or without sin. All Scripture tells us is that God "filled him with the Spirit of God." If you believe God wants to entirely change your life by the power of the Holy Spirit, this study guide is for you. God can use anybody to fulfill His purposes, and He wants to use you! This study is for anyone who wants to see relationships healed, self-esteem lifted, purpose revealed, clarity released, peace reigning, hope overflowing, and the goodness and faithfulness of God displayed.

Whoever you are, wherever you come from, this Bible study and my book

Unlimited: Experiencing the Fullness of God's Power in Your Life are for you! If you have tried for far too long and spent far too much of your valuable energy trying to manage everything going on in your life, I encourage you to surrender your strength to the indwelling presence and unlimited power of the Holy Spirit. Each part of this study is meant to leave you with a deeper understanding of the Holy Spirit and give you scriptural resources and practical applications to help unleash the unlimited power of the Holy Spirit in your life.

At the start of each week you will see a QR code like the following one directing you to a bonus video from me. You can use a smartphone to access this content, or you can visit unlimitedguide.info and click on the links to view the same bonus material.

In week 1 we will discover who the Holy Spirit is and what He provides for us. In weeks 2 to 5 we will discover that REST allows us to function in the fullness of the Holy Spirit. Each of those weeks will be devoted to one of these four principles: "Receive," "Empty and Fill," "Study Scripture and Pray," and "Trust the Spirit's Leading."

Then in week 6 we will discover the benefits of the Holy Spirit. The Holy Spirit is the only source of true satisfaction. Life's hardships and disappointments will drain you, but I am happy to report that the Holy Spirit's power is available to everybody, every day, and His power and His presence will never run out because they are *unlimited*!

SELF-REFLECTION

Before you begin this study in earnest, I want you to take a minute to reflect on what you already know and believe about the Holy Spirit by answering the following questions.

Do you have any knowledge of the Holy Spirit? If so, give a brief description of your knowledge.

_____

_____

Have you ever felt the tangible presence of the Holy Spirit? If so, what was your experience like?

_____

_____

_____

Are you afraid of the Holy Spirit? If so, what makes you feel that way?

_____

_____

_____

On pages 18–19 of *Unlimited*, I share that there are three groups of people in this world:

1. Those who don't know the Lord and have not received the Holy Spirit

2. Those who know the Lord and have received the Holy Spirit but have never completely surrendered to His lordship

3. Those who know the Lord and are controlled by the Holy Spirit

What attitude do you have regarding the Holy Spirit?

_____

_____

_____

On page 8 of *Unlimited*, I suggest there are three attitudes that can lead a person to disregard the Holy Spirit: ignorance (being unlearned or uninformed), indifference (lacking concern or viewing the Holy Spirit as unimportant), and indulgence (having an experience that is overly excessive and not based on biblical truths concerning the Holy Spirit).

Do you disregard the Holy Spirit? If so, which attitude do you find yourself leaning into most?

_____

_____

_____

I want you to revisit your answers to those questions at the end of this study. But before we go on, I want to draw your attention to a critical fact about the Holy Spirit that will affect everything we discuss going forward.

In Acts 2, the Holy Spirit was poured out on the day of Pentecost. Verse 2 says, "Suddenly there came from heaven a sound like a mighty rushing wind, and it filled the entire house where they were sitting." The noise drew a crowd of devout Jews who were in Jerusalem, and they were full of questions. The crowd was "from every nation under heaven" (v. 5)—Egypt, Asia, Rome, and elsewhere—yet they heard the disciples speaking in their native languages. They wondered, "What does this all mean?"

Peter explained that this moment had been prophesied throughout the Hebrew Scriptures. Jesus was the promised Messiah who would come and pour out His

Spirit on all people, and there was only one way to access this power. Peter said, "Repent and be baptized every one of you in the name of Jesus Christ for the forgiveness of your sins, and you will receive the gift of the Holy Spirit" (Acts 2:38).

The same is still true today. There is only one way to receive the gift of the Holy Spirit.

Friend, have you repented of your sins and turned to God? If not, please don't let one more minute pass. Until you take this crucial step, the Holy Spirit cannot be activated in your life.

If you haven't done so already, please use this simple prayer to ask Jesus into your life:

> *Lord Jesus, I am a sinner, and I am sorry for my sins. I'm so sorry, and I want to change. I believe You died on the cross as payment for my sins. I confess my sins to You right now. Come into my heart, Lord. Come into my life and forgive me. Thank You, Jesus, for forgiving me. Thank You for saving me!*

If you said that prayer, congratulations! You've just made the best decision of your life. Your sins are forgiven, and you are now part of the family of God. I encourage you to tell a pastor at your church so they can help you with your next steps as a believer. I also invite you to scan the following Flowcode or visit MadeNew.info to access several resources that will help you grow in your walk with Christ.

TAP INTO GOD'S POWER
madenew.info

Those who have accepted Jesus as Lord have received the Holy Spirit. Now, let's discover exactly what that means.

WHO IS THE HOLY SPIRIT?

TAP INTO GOD'S POWER
week1.unlimitedguide.info

AS WE BEGIN our study together, let's take a moment to ask the Lord to open our hearts and minds to receive from Him this week. Pray with me:

Lord, we want to know Your Spirit, who gives life. Open our eyes to understanding, open our hearts to behold the truths You have for us here, and open our ears to hear what Your plan is for us. Amen.

Now, let's get started!

DAY 1
THE HOLY SPIRIT IS OUR LIFE

The Spirit of God has made me, and the
breath of the Almighty gives me life.
—JOB 33:4

A S WE GO through this study, I want to make sure we have a mutual understanding of who the Holy Spirit is and what He does in our lives. So I want to begin by stating plainly that the Holy Spirit is a *person*. He is the third part of the Trinity, which is the Father, Son, and Holy Spirit. While that concept is hard to fully comprehend, it's true nonetheless. God is Three in One.

I would like to begin by asking you a couple of questions.

Who is the Holy Spirit to you?

_____

_____

What role does the Holy Spirit play in your life?

_____

_____

As Christians we worship God the Father, God the Son, and God the Holy Spirit. God is Three in One, and He wants a relationship with you. He wants you to relate to Him just like you'd relate to anyone you care deeply for.

But the Holy Spirit is a gentleman, and He does not go where He is not welcome. He will wait patiently for you to invite Him in. The Holy Spirit wants to be active in your life, but He will not force Himself on you.

3

With that in view, how is the Holy Spirit active in your life?

_____

_____

Second, I want us to understand that the Holy Spirit was *present in the beginning.*

> The earth was without form and void, and darkness was over the face of the deep. And the Spirit of God was hovering over the face of the waters.
> —GENESIS 1:2

Do you see the mention of the Holy Spirit in Genesis 1:2? What was He doing in this verse?

_____

_____

_____

The Hebrew word translated "Spirit" in Genesis 1:2 is *ruach.* It means "wind; by resemblance breath, i.e. a sensible (or even violent) exhalation."[1] The breath that was with God in the beginning is the same breath we are given upon receiving Jesus into our hearts as our Lord and Savior. In the New Testament, *Spirit* is the Greek word *pneuma.* It means "a current of air, i.e. breath (blast) or a breeze."[2] The root word is *pneō,* meaning "to breathe, to blow; of the wind; to breathe hard."[3]

Read Acts 2:2. Do you see the Holy Spirit in this verse? What form does He take?

_____

_____

In Acts 2:2 we see the Holy Spirit descend upon the disciples just as Jesus told them He would: "And suddenly there came from heaven a noise like a mighty rushing *wind*, and it filled the entire house where they were sitting" (emphasis added). The word *wind* here is literally translated "breath, breath of life."[4] In John 10:10 Jesus tells us, "I came that they may have *life* and have it abundantly" (emphasis added). The word translated "life" here means "of the absolute fullness of life, both essential and ethical, which belongs to God." It is "life real and genuine, a life active and vigorous, devoted to God" and "blessed."[5]

When the Holy Spirit came as a mighty, rushing breath of life, we were all given access to the gift of abundant living through the power of the Holy Spirit. We are now able to live lives that are real, genuine, and devoted to God, just as Jesus did when He walked this earth. The same Spirit that was hovering in Genesis 1:2 and waiting for God to speak lives inside those who have received Jesus. The Spirit is the "exhale" or "breath" of God. Those terms communicate action. When the Trinity is at work, things happen that are, in the language of Ephesians 3:20, "far more abundantly than all that we ask or think."

Next, I want us to understand that because He is a person, the Holy Spirit has a mind, a will, and emotions.

> How does knowing that the Holy Spirit is a person with a mind, a will, and emotions affect how you view Him? How might it affect how you interact with Him?
>
> _____
>
> _____
>
> _____
>
> Read Genesis 1:26. In whose likeness is mankind made?
>
> _____
>
> _____

Genesis 1:26 explains why humans are different from everything else God created: we are made in His image. Every human has a mind, a will, and emotions that make up the soul. And if humans were created in the image of God, the Holy Spirit must also have a mind, a will, and emotions. The Holy Spirit has a mind, for He is our Teacher (John 14:26). He has a will, for He desires to commune with you (2 Cor. 13:14). He has emotions, for Scripture tells us we can grieve, quench, resist, and blaspheme the Holy Spirit (Eph. 4:30; 1 Thess. 5:19; Acts 7:51; Matt. 12:31–32). The Bible also tells us the Spirit leads us to become more like Christ, and when we follow Him, we bear His fruit: "love, joy, peace, patience, kindness, goodness, faithfulness, gentleness, self-control" (Gal. 5:22–23).

While the Holy Spirit may be sensitive, His emotions are steady and right before God. We can look at Jesus' life and see that He, too, had emotions. He became angry but did not sin (Matt. 21). He grieved and even wept (John 11:35). He became indignant (Mark 10:14), He showed compassion (Matt. 9:36), and He experienced agony (Luke 22:44). Yet while Jesus had emotions, He was patient, respectful, and intentional. Keep in mind that the Holy Spirit is, in fact, the Spirit of Christ Himself. The same power, the same character, the same emotional capacity that was inside Jesus is now inside us!

Can you maintain steady emotions? Describe your emotions and how they change throughout the day.

_____

_____

_____

Do you let circumstances impact how you feel? If so, how?

_____

_____

What emotions do you often have that are not right or not pleasing to God?

_____

_____

_____

While some people think of God as stoic, He came in the form of a man and showed us He is anything but. He has a mind, a will, and emotions, and the Holy Spirit is now in us so that in our own experience of emotion we can respond in a manner that is pleasing to Him.

Last, the Holy Spirit has power. As Oswald Chambers once said, "The Spirit is the first power we practically experience, but the last power we come to understand."[6] This has been true in my own life. It was the Holy Spirit who stirred in my life when I was a young boy. The power of the Holy Spirit convicted my heart and led me to a moment of salvation. Today, having known and served the Lord for more than forty years, I still don't completely understand the all-consuming power of the Holy Spirit, but I continue learning about Him every day.

Through the Holy Spirit, God gives us all the same power and access that He gave His Son. In fact, when Jesus left the earth He promised to send the Holy Spirit, and He commissioned His disciples to reach the world.

Read Acts 1:8.

What will you receive?

_____

_____

When will you receive it?

_____

_____

What will be the result?

_____

_____

God is not a God of little or less but of the unlimited! Look to His Word and read His promises to those who put their hope in Him. This world will leave you hopeless and empty when you try to do everything on your own, but God will fill you with Holy Spirit power (a mighty, rushing breath of life) and relieve you of the burdens you carry. He offers living water that will flow into your soul and provide nourishment for all that seems dead in your life!

I pray the time you spent in this study guide today has left you with a better understanding of who the Holy Spirit is. And I pray that as you begin to understand that the Holy Spirit, God's very breath, lives inside you, you will become more confident about His role in your life and live the fully abundant life He has called you to!

DAY 2
THE HOLY SPIRIT IS OUR ADVOCATE

*I will instruct you and teach you in the way you should
go; I will counsel you with my eye upon you.*
—PSALM 32:8

AS WE BEGIN today's study, let's take a moment to pray:

*Jesus, we love You! Show us Your presence and help us to know
that You are advocating on our behalf every moment so others
can see You as we walk confidently in You! Amen.*

The word *advocate* is key, as the Holy Spirit serves as *our* Advocate. If you have accepted Jesus as your Savior, then you have access to the One who justifies you before the throne and pleads your innocence because of the blood Jesus shed for you. He also acknowledges you, and when the enemy tries to use your sin against you or to shame you, the Advocate is there to help you in your weakest moments, to be a voice on your behalf before God. He also advises, consults, and devises plans with us.

Read 1 John 2:1–2.

If we sin, who helps us?

_____

Who can receive that help?

_____

On what basis can we receive that help?

_____

The Greek word translated "advocate" in 1 John 2:1 is *paraklētos*, meaning "summoned, called to one's side, esp. called to one's aid; one who pleads another's cause before a judge, a pleader, counsel for defense, legal assistant; one who pleads another's cause with one, an intercessor; of the Holy Spirit destined to take the place of Christ with the apostles (after his ascension to the Father), to lead them to a deeper knowledge of the gospel truth, and give them divine strength needed to enable them to undergo trials and persecutions on behalf of the divine kingdom."[1]

The word *paraklētos* is also translated "comforter." An advocate comes along to help comfort someone else. To help illustrate this definition, consider how the judicial system helps children in foster care and adverse situations. When a child needs representation in the courts because of some form of abuse or other issue with the parents, a court-appointed special advocate (CASA) or a guardian ad litem (GAL) is appointed, depending on the situation and the age of the child. The CASA or GAL is legally an "advocate" for the child. This advocate's job is to meet with and listen to the child, to help the court understand the child's needs, and to plead for the best solution for the child. When the advocate meets with the child, they recognize that not every child wants someone to "fix" their problem; they just want to be heard.

What can a person say or do to show you they acknowledge you?

_____

_____

_____

Do you believe the Holy Spirit acknowledges you? Why or why not?

_____

_____

_____

In the CASA and GAL programs, the advocate may not always agree with the child, but they present the child's case and report the facts as the advocate sees it. As children of God, we have been given an Advocate called the Holy Spirit. He was sent by Jesus, and He is always there to listen to us, walk with us, and encourage us. He takes our deepest wounds, hurts, disappointments, challenges, and joys to our Father.

Whenever we are injured or need a shoulder to lean on, our Advocate is always beside us. Our Advocate is our aid and our divine strength. When life does not make sense or is too painful for words, He is the One who leads us into a deeper knowledge of the truth. He is the forgiver of our sins and a lover of our soul, the One who escorts us to the very throne of God.

Do you need an advocate right now? If so, what do you need your advocate to do?

_____

_____

_____

Do you want someone to listen to you? What would you like your advocate to know?

_____

_____

Do you need a counselor to defend you against an accuser? What or whom do you need to be defended from?

_____

_____

_____

Do you need someone to be called to your aid? In what areas are you weak and in need of healing?

_____

_____

_____

Do you need divine strength or deeper knowledge of the gospel truth? What is something in your life that does not make sense and that only God can help you with?

_____

_____

_____

Is there sin in your life that you need God to forgive? Write your sin here and accept the forgiveness that is given to you.

_____

_____

_____

When the Bible uses the word *Advocate* to describe the Holy Spirit, I can't help but think about how God sent the Holy Spirit to live inside us because of His great love for us. The Holy Spirit takes up residence inside us to help us finish the race that has been set before us. We have an enemy who is an accuser and a liar and does not want us to be fully devoted to Jesus. God gave us the Holy Spirit as our Advocate because He knows that at times we will certainly feel alone, unheard, and insignificant. People will injure us or not acknowledge us or our feelings. No matter what we are going through, we never have to walk alone because God gave us an Advocate as a guarantee.

Read 2 Corinthians 5:5.

What is our guarantee, or what is given in earnest, according to this verse?

Do you see the word *guarantee* or *earnest* in that verse? This reminds me of when my wife, Barbara, and I were first married. I liked to shop at a store called Goody's. I went there one day to buy Barbara a dress, but I didn't have enough money to pay for it. Back in those days stores would offer a program called layaway. You could get the item you wanted to purchase, put some earnest money toward it, and make incremental payments until the price had been paid in full. Every time I went by Goody's, I would stop and give them more money toward Barbara's dress until it was paid for in full. Once the dress was paid for, I could take it home and give it to my bride.

God put down "earnest money" for you and me in the form of the Holy Spirit, and our Advocate is our guarantee that we are going to make it through whatever we face in life. Our Advocate is there to walk with us, and He will encourage us until we are on the other side of our struggle.

Read Romans 8:26–27.

Who helps us in our weakness?

When we don't know how to pray, what does the Spirit do?

_____

Whose will does the Spirit seek?

_____

If you feel like you do not know how to pray, you are in good company. The apostle Paul wrote the Book of Romans, including the passage you just read, as well as most of the books in the New Testament. And he wasn't the only one in the Bible who needed help with prayer.

Read Matthew 6:9–13.

Who is teaching here?

_____

Whom is this person teaching?

_____

The disciples were with Jesus every day, they heard Him pray, and they watched Him go away regularly to pray, yet they needed Jesus to teach them how to pray. Just as Jesus was willing to teach His disciples, our Advocate, the Holy Spirit, is with us to teach us to pray. (We will spend more time on this in week 4.)

We have an Advocate who is with us in our times of deepest need. He is there to listen to us, acknowledge us, and walk with us through every circumstance of our lives. He is our great Defender, and He is willing to fight every battle in and through us. God created this world and sent His Son into it so we never have to be alone. He sent us an Advocate to plead our case before the righteous Judge. I hope this gives you confidence that you are accepted and fully loved by God.

DAY 3
THE HOLY SPIRIT IS OUR HELPER

But the Helper, the Holy Spirit, whom the Father will
send in my name, he will teach you all things and bring
to your remembrance all that I have said to you.

—JOHN 14:26

BEFORE WE APPROACH God's Word today, let's pause and ask the Lord to lead us and open our minds and hearts to what He has for us today:

We pray that You will speak to us and through us today! All we want to do today is honor and glorify You! I pray that You will clear the distractions so our minds and hearts can hear what You have for us today. Amen.

When I first started following the Lord and knew I was called to be a preacher, there were many things I didn't know. For instance, I called the Book of Psalms "Spasms"; I pronounced the Book of Job (ˈjōb) as job (ˈjäb), like it was a place of employment; and I thought the epistles were the apostles' wives.

Have you ever read the Bible and thought, "I don't understand what I am reading," or, "This doesn't make any sense!"?

Here is what I have found: the Holy Spirit is our Helper when we do not understand Scripture or spiritual things. I have an example that may help us understand. I have been married to Barbara for forty years, and through that time she has prepared a lot of meals. If you said, "Benny, give me the ingredients of every single meal Mrs. Barbara has cooked in the last forty years," I know I could not do that. I believe I received strength and nourishment from every meal. But I cannot tell you every detail of every meal that has been provided for me over time.

It is the same way when I read my Bible. I may not understand everything I read, but what I do know is I have received spiritual health and nourishment from the time I have spent studying my Bible. And I trust that the Holy Spirit will bring Scripture to my memory when I need it.

Read 2 Timothy 3:16–17.

How is all Scripture created?

_____

_____

What is Scripture profitable for?

_____

_____

The Greek word translated "inspired" in 2 Timothy 3:16 (NASB) is *theopneustos*, and it means "divinely breathed in: given by inspiration of God."[1] God breathed His Word. You receive the breath of God when you spend time in His Word.

We all need help sometimes. We need someone beside us to gently point us to wisdom and truth and help us see the beauty of God's Word so we can hear His voice and move in His direction.

Read 1 John 2:27.

Where does the Holy Spirit live?

_____

What does the Holy Spirit teach you?

_____

What is everything the Holy Spirit teaches?

_____

In whom are we to remain or abide?

First John 2:27 speaks of the anointing: "But the anointing that you received from him abides in you, and you have no need that anyone should teach you. But as his anointing teaches you about everything, and is true, and is no lie— just as it has taught you, abide in him." The Greek word used here is *chrisma*, meaning "an unguent or smearing, i.e. (figuratively) the special endowment of the Holy Spirit: anointing, unction."[2]

Bible teacher Warren Wiersbe had this to say about the anointing:

> The word anoint reminds us of the Old Testament practice of pouring oil on the head of a person being set apart for special service....A New Testament Christian is anointed, not with literal oil, but by the Spirit of God—an anointing that sets him apart for his ministry as one of God's priests (1 Peter 2:5, 9). It is not necessary for you to pray for "an anointing of the Spirit"; if you are a Christian, you have already received this special anointing. This anointing "abides in us" and therefore does not need to be imparted to us.[3]

Because the Holy Spirit abides in us, we have a Teacher who is constantly with us to show us what He wants us to see and learn. We are capable of reading Scripture, and then the Holy Spirit brings to light what is helpful for us in our time of greatest need. We have the Spirit in us who will distinguish the truth from lies. He is our Protector against ignorance and deception, He helps us get where God is leading us, and He gives us power to overcome every obstacle we face!

God is a divine, spiritual being, which means our finite, human minds cannot comprehend His thoughts, ways, or words. Without the help of the Holy Spirit we cannot know God or understand the magnitude of who He is.

Read Ephesians 1:17–21.

Who does God give us?

What do we gain by having spiritual wisdom and insight?

_____

_____

In Ephesians 1:18 Paul tells us that the Spirit helps us *know* the hope to which He has called us. When life is overwhelming and it feels like a situation is hopeless, remember God sent us the Holy Spirit to help us. The Holy Spirit gives us the wisdom to know God better as we grow in our relationship with Him. When we know God better, we begin to trust His heart for us, and when we trust His heart for us, we act in the hope that is promised to us. That is a miracle. God did not leave us here on earth alone to figure life out by ourselves! He sent us a Helper—the Holy Spirit!

Read 1 Corinthians 2:10.

Who revealed things to us?

_____

What was the Spirit's function in God's revelation?

_____

The Spirit searches "even the depths of God." If we want to know and understand God better, and if we want to have a trusting relationship with Him, we need a Helper who searches "everything." This word is *pas*, and it means "all, any, every, the whole: always(-s), any (one), daily, ever, every (one, way)...thoroughly, whatsoever, whole, whosoever."[4] If we need discernment, we need a Helper who searches everything. If we need wisdom, we need a Helper who searches everything. If we need truth, we need a Helper who searches everything! We all need help. Why wouldn't we use the Helper who has our best interest in mind, knows the best plan for our lives, and searches everything to give us hope?

The Holy Spirit wants to help you, strengthen you, give you wisdom, instruct you, and so much more. Without the Holy Spirit enlightening our understanding we cannot comprehend the eternal value and application of God's Word for each of us personally. Because of the Holy Spirit's power to help people understand the Bible, you and I can read the exact same scripture and gain completely different insights. When we let the Holy Spirit guide our understanding of the Bible, we gain knowledge far beyond anything the world could ever teach.

The Holy Spirit wants to come alongside you in your Christian walk to help you in both times of need and times of plenty. The Holy Spirit does not want you to take this walk of faith without wisdom or discernment. The Holy Spirit's will is for God's perfect plan to come to fruition for you. The foundation of His will is not self-serving but Christ-serving! When you choose to surrender your will to His, He will help you fulfill your purpose of becoming more like Jesus.

THE HOLY SPIRIT IS OUR LIVING WATER

If anyone thirsts, let him come to me and drink. Whoever believes in me, as the Scripture has said, "Out of his heart will flow rivers of living water." Now this he said about the Spirit.

—JOHN 7:37–39

LET'S TAKE A moment and ask the Holy Spirit to give us wisdom and discernment as we approach His Word and what He would like us to learn from Him today. Pray this prayer with me:

Jesus, we bow our heads and our hearts in Your presence. Find anything that would hinder our time with You today. Please open our hearts to receive Your wisdom and discernment as we approach our time with You. Amen.

The Holy Spirit is so beautiful and gives us so much life! Jesus came to take away our sins and reconcile us to God, but when He ascended to heaven, He did not leave us without help. In John 10:10 Jesus reminds us that He came "that they may have life and have it abundantly." One of the ways Jesus provided that abundant life was by giving us living water through the Holy Spirit.

Some of us are spiritually dehydrated, meaning we are not being filled with the living water that can only be provided through a relationship with Jesus Christ. D. L. Moody was known for praying that God would fill him with the Holy Spirit. He said, "The fact is, we are leaky vessels, and we have to keep right under the fountain all the time to keep full of Christ, and so have fresh supply."[1] If we are not praying for a fresh filling of the Holy Spirit, which is our living water, we will inevitably become spiritually dehydrated.

What does spiritual dehydration look like?

_____

_____

_____

Some people have never asked Jesus into their hearts; therefore, they have never been filled with the Holy Spirit. Another way spiritual dehydration surfaces is when we give in to temptations and thought patterns that are detrimental to our overall spiritual health. Another example is when we lose our appetite for seeking God and do not seek truth and wisdom from His Word. Confusion eventually takes over because we become so much like the world that we cannot differentiate between truth and lies.

Let's look at the story of the Samaritan woman at Jacob's well in John 4:5–30. Take a moment to read this passage.

Notice the time of day. It was the sixth hour, meaning it was in the heat of the day. Notice also that the woman went to the well alone. This tells us she was not accepted by the women in her community, because the women typically visited the well together early in the cool of the day. By geography we also know the woman would have had to walk up a hill daily to get back to Samaria with her water. She would not have chosen to get water at the well when it was hot.

This woman was alone at the well at a time when she would have been thirsty because of the heat, and that's when she came upon Jesus. He asked her for a drink, and she responded by telling Him that He was a Jew and should not be speaking with her because she was a Samaritan. Let us look at verse 10:

> Jesus answered her, "If you knew the gift of God, and who it is that is saying to you, 'Give me a drink,' you would have asked him, and he would have given you living water."

To add more context to this conversation, let's look at a few more verses.

In Jeremiah 2:13, who is the fountain of living waters?

_____

_____

In John 7:37, what is Jesus claiming?

_____

_____

_____

In John 4:14, what do you think Jesus wanted the
Samaritan woman to understand?

_____

_____

_____

Jesus was asking the Samaritan woman to exchange her life for His—to surrender her life to Him. In verse 14 Jesus described the water He gives, saying, "whoever drinks of the water that I will give him will never be thirsty again. The water that I will give him will become in him a spring of water welling up to eternal life."

In verses 13–15 Jesus uses the words *thirst* or *thirsty* three times. This is the Greek word *dipsaō*, which means "to suffer thirst, suffer from thirst" and refers to those "who painfully feel their want of, and eagerly long for, those things by which the soul is refreshed, supported, strengthened."[2] Thirst represents the spiritual need and longing everyone has, and only Jesus can give us lasting satisfaction.

In verses 13 and 14, when Jesus tells the woman to "drink," the Greek word being used is *pinō*, and it means "to receive into the soul what serves to refresh, strengthen, nourish it unto life eternal."[3] When we are thirsty, we want, long, search, and reach, just like the woman at the well did. Jesus beckons us to come, drink, and receive what He serves to refresh and nourish us into eternal life! Notice Jesus did not use the past tense "drank" in His conversation with the Samaritan woman, nor did He tell her she must take only one drink. He invited her to come drink repeatedly from the water He provides.

> Describe a time when you needed spiritual refreshment and hydration. (Maybe you feel that way right now.) What caused you to become so depleted?

_____

_____

_____

> How would receiving the living water Jesus described change this situation?

_____

_____

_____

Have you ever been out in nature and seen a fresh spring? Water literally comes up from the ground. It is bubbling and never seems to dry up. Spring water runs underneath the ground until it finds a crevice to come out, and then it continually flows from that place. Jesus is telling the Samaritan woman (and us!) that He is the living water. If we come seeking Him and receive His gift of the Holy Spirit, our deepest times of "drought" will become like fresh springs bubbling up and never running dry. Jesus did not ask the woman to take the water. He said, "Whoever drinks of the water that I will give him will never be thirsty again." We must receive what He is giving us.

Jesus went to Samaria—(John 4:4 tells us "He *had* to pass through Samaria" [emphasis added])—specifically to tell the woman that He was the living water she needed and her deepest wounds, wants, and desires could be healed and fulfilled because He was the Messiah she had been waiting for. He is the living water that satisfies her deepest thirst. After her conversation with Jesus the woman left her water jar to go tell others what she had found. She had come to the well to draw water to quench her thirst, and after having an encounter with Jesus and surrendering her life to Him, she could not wait to tell others about Him.

What do you thirst for that only Jesus can provide?

_____

_____

What do you need to surrender? Is it your life? Your schedule? Your loved ones? Your reputation?

_____

_____

What is in your "water jar" that you need to leave behind? What do you bring to Jesus daily that you need to leave at His feet so you can live in freedom and then tell others what He has done for you?

_____

_____

_____

Psalm 36:7–9 says, "How precious is your steadfast love, O God! The children of mankind take refuge in the shadow of your wings. They feast on the abundance of your house, and you give them drink from the river of your delights. For with you is the fountain of life; in your light do we see light."

Having living water means you never have to thirst again. You never need to return to your water jar. God has living water in abundance! Having living water means no spiritual need will be left unmet. It means you have access to a resource that is always flowing and available. Through the power of the Holy Spirit we can experience eternal life and peace that passes all understanding.

Jesus told the Samaritan woman, "Everyone who drinks of this water..." (John 4:13). What does God require us to do in order to receive the Holy Spirit? We must simply come and drink the living water daily.

DAY 5
THE HOLY SPIRIT IS TRUTH

*When the Spirit of truth comes, he will guide you into all the truth,
for he will not speak on his own authority, but whatever he hears he
will speak, and he will declare to you the things that are to come. He
will glorify me, for he will take what is mine and declare it to you.*

—John 16:13–14

PLEASE STOP FOR just a moment and simply breathe. As you inhale and exhale, ask the Holy Spirit to help you see what God wants to show you today. Pray with me:

Jesus, thank You for Your presence! Holy Spirit, give us eyes to see what You would like for us to see today! We come to You seeking Your truth, and we believe that You will show us! Amen.

Jesus was always careful to give His disciples the right amount of truth at the best time. This is always the mark of a great teacher. The Holy Spirit follows the same principle: He teaches us the truths we need to know, when we need them, when we are ready to receive them. Let's look at this principle at work in the account of Jesus teaching Nicodemus.

Read John 3:1–21.

Nicodemus was a prominent figure within the Jewish Sanhedrin and a leading member of the Pharisaic religious order. He came to see Jesus, curious about the popular and controversial rabbi he was hearing so much about in Jerusalem and the temple. So he asked to meet with Jesus—in the dark. He did not want his association with Jesus to be publicly known.

Describe a time when you felt tempted to keep your association with Jesus hidden. How did you respond?

_____

_____

_____

As you are working through this study guide, are you coming in the dark like Nicodemus? Do you want your association with Jesus hidden? Why? Are you curious, like Nicodemus?

_____

_____

_____

How does having a relationship with Jesus affect your work? Your marriage? Other relationships?

_____

_____

_____

How does having a relationship with Jesus impact your finances or other parts of your life?

_____

_____

_____

Read John 3:16.

Whom did God so love?

_____

_____

_____

What or whom did God give because of His love?

_____

_____

_____

What is the *only* thing any person must do to receive this gift?

_____

_____

_____

What happens when a person does that one thing?

_____

_____

_____

The Holy Spirit, the Spirit of Truth, has come to reveal to each of us that all we must do is believe God's Word! The Spirit of Truth shows us that God is not a harsh judge with a list of rules that can never be achieved. He does not require us to be perfect in order to receive His love. The Spirit of Truth calls us into the light so we can be free from our own personal darkness and know that we are eternally accepted and loved by the One who so desperately wants a relationship with us. The Holy Spirit, the Spirit of Truth, is calling *you* to embrace this reality.

Read John 3:19–21.

> What do you think Jesus was saying to Nicodemus? What do you draw from that conclusion?

When Jesus is speaking to Nicodemus about stepping into the light, He is not taking a jab at Nicodemus' nighttime visit (at least, not exclusively). Jesus' words are meant for Nicodemus, the disciples who were with Him, and everyone who would ever read about this conversation that occurred under the cloak of night. His words are a call to introspection, to take stock of what is really in our hearts—and what is not.

This kind of inward reflection can be scary and difficult. To see ourselves as God sees us will call to light our true heart and challenge us to align it with the Spirit of Truth. Our spiritual insufficiency and moral decay will be laid out before us, and that is so painful to see. But it is also one of the most freeing experiences. Because the Holy Spirit is Truth, He already knows what dwells inside each of us, and He loves us anyway. Where there is Truth, there is healing. Where the healing occurs, there is freedom.

> Take stock of what the Spirit of Truth is telling you about yourself now. What is He saying to you?

What do you need to bring into the light?

_____

_____

What do you need to release so Jesus can bring you freedom?

_____

_____

_____

If your responses showed you that you feel insufficient to complete the task Jesus has put in front of you, take comfort in the fact that Jesus was showing Nicodemus the very same thing.

Look up Lamentations 3:40 and write it here.

_____

_____

Now look up 1 John 1:9 and write it here.

_____

_____

The Spirit of Truth speaks truth to lies and helps us differentiate between darkness and light. The Spirit of Truth awakens us to the truth in Scripture and gives us the courage to step out in faith when we feel ill-equipped and unprepared. When we are led by the Spirit of Truth, we become spiritually awake and fully alive!

In the account of Nicodemus in John 3 we are not told Nicodemus believed

Jesus was the Messiah or that he became a follower of Jesus. But when we read further in Scripture, we notice in John 19:39 that after Jesus died on the cross, "Nicodemus also, who earlier had come to Jesus by night, came bringing a mixture of myrrh and aloes, about seventy-five pounds in weight." This time Nicodemus did not come in the dark. He showed up in the middle of the day and brought seventy-five pounds of myrrh and aloes, which would be used to anoint Jesus for burial. There was nothing hidden this time. Nicodemus risked his reputation by touching a dead body so close to the Sabbath, thus making himself ceremonially unclean.

I believe we can conclude that Nicodemus listened to the Spirit of Truth and surrendered his life to Jesus. Nicodemus was changed because he interacted with the person of Jesus and accepted truth.

What does it mean to accept the Spirit of Truth?

_____

_____

_____

What often prevents you from receiving the Spirit of Truth?

_____

_____

_____

Look up 2 Corinthians 5:17 and write it here.

_____

_____

_____

The Spirit of Truth not only convicts us of the darkness in our hearts but also leads us to the light. If you believe Jesus came, died on a cross, was resurrected on the third day, and ascended to heaven, you are a new creation in Christ. All those things you wrote earlier that are darkness can now be transformed by the light of Truth. With the Spirit of Truth dwelling inside us, we can do things that once seemed impossible. He will direct us and lead us exactly where the Lord wants us to go.

REST: RECEIVE THE HOLY SPIRIT

TAP INTO
GOD'S POWER
week2.unlimitedguide.info

N WEEKS 2–4 I use an acronym to help us remember how to activate the Holy Spirit in our lives: REST.

1. *Receive* all that the Holy Spirit offers.

2. *Empty* and allow yourself to be filled with the Spirit.

3. *Study* Scripture and pray.

4. *Trust* the Spirit's leading; transform your mind.

Before we begin this week's study on how to *receive* what the Holy Spirit desires for us, let's take a moment to stop and thank the Holy Spirit for what He plans to reveal:

Holy Spirit, we can't conceive anything You have for us on our own, but You have already gone before us and cleared the path to help us discern Your truths. We invite You to do something here with us today. And for all You do, we praise You. We pray this in Jesus' name. Amen.

DAY 1
HOW DO I RECEIVE THE HOLY SPIRIT?

Behold, I stand at the door and knock. If anyone hears My voice and opens the door, I will come in to him and dine with him, and he with Me.
—REVELATION 3:20, NKJV

A s I SAID earlier in this study guide, the Holy Spirit is a gentleman. A gentleman never enters where he is not invited; he is courteous and honorable. The Holy Spirit will never force you to receive Him. He is willing to wait for you to accept what He has to offer—abundant life.

John 7:39 (NASB) says, "But this He spoke of the Spirit, whom those who believed in Him were to receive." The word *receive* here is *lambanō* in the Greek. It means "to take with the hand, lay hold of, any person or thing in order to use it…to take up a thing to be carried; to take upon oneself."[1] Jesus was telling us that He is the living water (John 7:38), and we read later in John 7 that Jesus was speaking of the Spirit, the One we are to "take" and "lay hold of," and who is "to be carried."[2] We are asked to receive the gift of the Holy Spirit. He has offered; we are recipients.

Read Acts 2:38. What must we do before we can receive this gift?

_____

_____

Read Acts 2:39. Who is the promise of the Holy Spirit for?

_____

_____

How have you received the gift of the Holy Spirit? Have you received Him excitedly or with disinterest?

_____

_____

_____

Do you think the Holy Spirit is for someone else and not for you? Have you discarded the Holy Spirit in your life?

_____

_____

_____

John 1:12 (NASB) says, "But as many as received Him, to them He gave the right to become children of God, even to those who believe in His name." The first thing we should do to entrust ourselves to the Holy Spirit is receive. We must receive all that God has in store for us—and no one can do that for us. What is John 1:12 saying we need to believe? That Jesus was born of a virgin, was the perfect sacrifice for our sin, died on the cross, was buried and raised to life on the third day, and ascended to the right hand of God. If we believe that, we can receive the Holy Spirit.

When we receive the Holy Spirit, we are given access to the same power, wisdom, discernment, truth, and light that Jesus had when He walked on the earth. But God gives us free will. He offers us everything; we get to choose whether we receive it. In Joshua 24:15 the Lord told His people to "choose this day whom you will serve." In 1 Kings 18:21 Elijah told the people of Israel the same thing: "How long will you go limping between two different opinions? If the LORD is God, follow him; but if Baal, then follow him." Jesus tells us in the Gospels that He has come to be our Living Water, Bread of Life, eternal life, and peace. Choose to receive Him. Choose to believe Him. Choose today whom you will serve.

I would like to show you something else the Bible says.

Read Ephesians 1:13. What happened after you believed?

_____

_____

Now read 2 Corinthians 1:21–22. What happens after we are established in Christ and anointed?

_____

_____

_____

The word *sealed* in 2 Corinthians 1:22 (KJV) is *sphragizō*, and it means "to stamp (with a signet or private mark) for security or preservation (literally or figuratively); by implication, to keep secret, to attest: (set a, set to) seal up, stop… to set a seal upon, mark with a seal…for security: from Satan."[3]

What is your response to the guarantee in 2 Corinthians 1:21–22? Are you excited about it? Are you doubtful? Are you hopeful?

_____

_____

_____

When you receive the Holy Spirit, you begin to understand truths in His Word you may have never seen. When you receive the Holy Spirit, you gain discernment and the power to conquer any sin in your life. Receiving the Holy Spirit allows you access to the throne of God and to a power that is "able to do far more abundantly than all that we ask or think" (Eph. 3:20). I pray that you choose today to receive *all* He has to offer. Receive your seal!

DAY 2
ASK

*Ask, and it will be given to you; seek, and you will find; knock, and
it will be opened to you. For everyone who asks receives, and the
one who seeks finds, and to the one who knocks it will be opened.*

—MATTHEW 7:7–8

LET'S BEGIN TODAY by praying Psalm 51:10–12 (NLT), asking God to create in us a clean heart:

*In the words of David, "Create in me a clean heart, O God. Renew
a loyal spirit within me. Do not banish me from your presence, and
don't take your Holy Spirit from me. Restore to me the joy of your
salvation, and make me willing to obey you." Amen.*

Today we will continue to learn how to receive the Holy Spirit by addressing something that is simple but sometimes surprisingly hard to do: *ask.*
Read Matthew 7:7–8.

What happens when you ask?

_____

_____

_____

Who gets denied when they ask?

_____

_____

Perhaps you are thinking, "Benny, I have asked for a lot of things from God, and He has not answered any of them!" Once again, we need to look at the original language to make sure we understand what Jesus is telling us in Matthew 7:7–8. The word translated "ask" in this passage is *aiteō*, which means "to ask, beg, call for, crave, desire, require."[1]

Here is an example: I often ask for Diet Mountain Dew. I have a desire for it; I crave it. Some people who spend time with me may tell you that I *require* it.

What is something you crave, desire, or require and would beg for?

_____

_____

How do you feel when you have not had that product in a specified amount of time?

_____

_____

_____

You should ask to receive the Holy Spirit with the same intensity with which you seek the item you just described.

Read Luke 11:13.

If you are a parent, do you like to give good gifts to your children? Why or why not?

_____

_____

_____

What would you consider a good gift to be?

_____

_____

_____

Whom does the Father give the Holy Spirit to?

_____

_____

_____

My daughter, Savannah Abigail, once took a job in Columbia, Missouri. When Barbara and I went to help her move, my daughter told me she wanted a grill. I asked her if there was a Walmart nearby, and she told me there was one about a mile down the road off the expressway. We drove to Walmart in our small rental car and found a gas grill that was already put together. You need to know that I do not put things together—because the item would never work again. I bought her that grill that was already assembled and I took it outside, only to find that it wouldn't fit in our little rental car. I went back inside to see if anyone could help me get to Savannah Abigail's new place with her new grill, and apparently no one had a truck.

It was so cold outside, I told Savannah Abigail to give me her coat. She tried to talk me out of walking the grill on the expressway back to her place, but I would not let her talk me out of it. I walked that gas grill down the expressway in the very frigid temperatures so my little girl could have a grill. Can I tell you something? If I would go to those lengths to give a gas grill to my daughter, how much more will God do for us?

Read Matthew 7:11. Our heavenly Father wants to give us the *best* gifts! He sent His Son to die on the cross and then gave us yet another gift after Jesus ascended to heaven! What is that gift? The same power Jesus had access to while He was on the earth.

God does not want us to think, "Whatever," when it comes to receiving the Holy Spirit. He wants us to beg, crave, desire, and require the Holy Spirit's presence in our lives. Unfortunately most of us have to take some hard knocks before we reach that point.

> What situation did it take for you to ask Jesus into your life? (By receiving Jesus, you receive the Holy Spirit.)

_____

_____

> If you have not reached that point, what do you think it would take?

_____

_____

Scripture tells you that you are worthy of all that Jesus offers you. Let's look to Scripture for evidence.

Read Luke 12:32.

> What does God find pleasure in giving you?

_____

_____

Read Romans 8:16–17.

> What does the Holy Spirit bear witness to?

_____

_____

That makes us heirs of whom?

_____

_____

_____

Read 1 Peter 2:9.

List all the adjectives this scripture uses to describe you.

_____

_____

_____

Which ones do you believe are true of you?

_____

_____

_____

If you do not believe any of these words describe you, why?

_____

_____

_____

Look up Ephesians 2:10 and write it here.

_____

_____

How hard or easy is it for you to believe this verse? What makes it easy or difficult?

_____

_____

_____

Brothers and sisters, I want you to hear God's heart. It does not matter what other people tell you. It does not matter what lies you tell yourself. It does not matter what you believe your life circumstances say about you or the choices you have made. God created you with His own hands; He says you are "fearfully and wonderfully made" (Ps. 139:14). He created only one of you, and He made you with a purpose in mind. That plan is to reach others for His glory and to further His kingdom.

What would it take for you to believe that all God's Word says about you is true?

_____

_____

_____

Friend, it *is* true! If God says it, you can believe it! Once you have hope that it *could* be true, you have taken a huge step. You are on your way to a life-giving experience with the Holy Spirit. He will help you shatter strongholds and lies the enemy has used against you for years.

How do we gain access to the Holy Spirit? All we must do is ask. You can simply say these words: "Holy Spirit, please open my eyes to the truth." Once you truly crave, desire, and require the Holy Spirit to have full access to your life, get ready to experience a peace that passes all understanding and begin the greatest adventure you could ever imagine! I am praying for you, my friend!

DAY 3
OBEY

If we live by the Spirit, let us also keep in step with the Spirit.
—GALATIANS 5:25

YOU HAVE DONE some really good work this week! I am proud of you! Before we tackle the material today, let's ask the Holy Spirit to open our hearts to receive more of His best for us. Pray with me:

Holy Spirit, I pray right now that You would open our hearts to receive more of Your best for us. Allow us to be honest with ourselves and receive all that You have for us today. We pray this prayer in Jesus' name. Amen.

The word *obedience* brings up different feelings for each of us depending on our upbringing and life circumstances. For some it can feel like an oppressive word that takes them back to harsh rules and discipline. It reminds some of pointless rules that are stifling instead of life-giving and fulfilling. For others obedience brings feelings of "I can never measure up; I'm not good enough," because "obeying God" took precedence over developing a healthy relationship with Him and left them feeling isolated and alone. For others obedience feels like a threat to their independence and rubs like sandpaper against their need for autonomy and self-reliance.

This kind of obedience is not what our loving Father has in store for us. Our Father is good and does not lack affection. He is not legalistic or oppressive. Our Father *does* set healthy boundaries and instructions out of a heart that is tender toward us. He desires for us to live our best lives. Obedience to God is not Him saying no; it is His best yes. When we obey God we are saying, "I trust You no matter how the circumstances seem because You love me and have my best interests in mind."

I love my wife, Barbara, and I believe she has my best interests in mind. When Barbara asks me to do something for her, I want to because I love her. When we obey the Holy Spirit, we open ourselves up to an ocean of grace that leads us to His unbridled blessing and abundance! You want to know what that feels like? Freedom and wholeness! Obedience is the alpha and omega of how we hear from God. It is the key that unlocks all the blessings God has for us.

Read Jesus' words in John 14:21.

How do we show our love for Jesus?

_____

_____

If we love Jesus, who are we loved by?

_____

_____

Do you say you love Jesus but go around either unknowledgeable of God's Word or just ignoring His Word? If so, why do you think that is? Why is the way you claim to honor God in your heart out of alignment with the Word God has given to you?

_____

_____

Write John 14:21 here.

_____

_____

What will be manifested to us if we have God's commandments and keep them?

_____

_____

The Greek word translated "manifest" here is *emphanizō*, which means "to exhibit (in person) or disclose (by words): appear, declare (plainly), inform, (will) manifest, shew, signify."[1] When we see God as He really is, our faith grows and our healing occurs. We grow in wisdom and discernment, live as victors instead of victims, have peace, and experience the abundant life Jesus promised us. By obeying God's Word and listening to the Holy Spirit, things that once did not make sense become clear, and following the Holy Spirit becomes an adventure. If you want this kind of life, say this prayer with me:

> *Father, open my heart and mind to follow the Holy Spirit and be obedient to You. Keep me in right standing with You so I may experience Your presence and live the life You have planned for me. Thank You for loving me!*

A heart that is submissive and tender toward God and His Word is one that is postured to continually discern the Holy Spirit's leading and distinguish it from the voices of the enemy, fear, and pride, which seek to deter us from doing God's will. To receive all that the Holy Spirit wants to do in our lives, we must be obedient to Him.

As believers, many of us intend to follow the Holy Spirit and obey God's Word. What gets in the way of your obedience to God?

_____

_____

_____

Have you ever decided to follow your own voice instead of the still, small voice of God? How did that work out for you? What would it take for you to follow the Holy Spirit instead of your own voice?

_____

_____

_____

Our hearts are stubborn, and the world tells us that if we don't take care of ourselves, nobody will. Are you willing to set yourself aside to obey the Holy Spirit in your life so you can live in the fullness of what God has called you to?

_____

_____

_____

How would it change your life if the Holy Spirit were to manifest in and through you in a greater measure?

_____

_____

_____

If you want the Holy Spirit to have full access to your life, you must be willing to obey everything He tells you to do, which will put you in a posture to hear Him. This one thing, obedience, will require courage and patience. It will require you not doing what the world tells you to do, to be in the world but not of the world (John 17:14). But it will lead you to freedom in Jesus!

How can you posture yourself to let the Holy Spirit search your heart further so He can reveal the hard places that keep you from obeying Him fully?

_____

_____

_____

Are you willing to let the Holy Spirit soften the hard areas of your heart? Why or why not?

_____

_____

_____

When I think of practicing obedience, I look to the Bible to see others who have gone before me and were obedient in the most difficult of circumstances. Let's look at Abraham for an example.

Look up Genesis 22:1–18 and read what God asked Abraham to do.

Do you think Abraham wanted to do this? Why or why not?

_____

_____

_____

Who was Abraham trusting?

_____

Do you trust God like Abraham did? Why or why not?

_____

_____

_____

How do you think trusting God like Abraham did would benefit you?

_____

_____

_____

How did Abraham show his trust?

_____

_____

How was Abraham's obedience rewarded?

_____

_____

I love that when God spoke to Abraham in Genesis 22, Abraham responded by saying, "Here I am" (vv. 1, 11). Abraham was in a posture to hear God. I also love that we do not see Abraham questioning God when He promised that Abraham would be the "father of many nations" even though he and Sarah had no children (Gen. 17:4–6, KJV). I also love that Abraham did not hesitate in obeying God when He asked him to sacrifice his promised son in Genesis 22. His response was immediate obedience (v. 3), worship (v. 5), and complete trust

(v. 8). The result was God providing a substitute sacrifice (v. 13) and Abraham being blessed (vv. 17–18).

God wasn't only willing to sacrifice His Son, Jesus—He did so willingly. No one else has loved us that much. Why should our hearts desire to obey the Holy Spirit? Because He loves us and wants His best for us.

Many of us are so bound by selfish desires and past hurts that having a trusting relationship with God seems impossible. Walking in obedience to the Holy Spirit is the only way such a relationship is possible. When we walk in a trusting relationship with God and are obedient to His Word, other people will find it irresistible.

The Holy Spirit desires to have an intimate relationship with you so you can walk confidently in who He created you to be. My friend, in order to walk in the obedience that gives freedom and life, we must trust the Holy Spirit—and this obedience is always followed by a blessing. Will you choose to obey the Holy Spirit today?

DAY 4

PRAISE

This people I have formed for Myself; they shall declare My praise.
—Isaiah 43:21, nkjv

WELCOME BACK! As we approach God's Word today, let's take a moment to thank the Holy Spirit for meeting us here:

Holy Spirit, I love You! Thank You for meeting us here today. Reveal to us what You have for us! Jesus, I pray that Your presence will lead us to praise that honors You alone. For what You are doing here today, we will praise You—for all of it! Amen.

Remember, we are taking time this week to focus on how we *receive* the Holy Spirit. One of my favorite ways to receive the Holy Spirit each day is to welcome the Spirit in with praise! There is a reason the sound crew at church keeps my microphone off during worship each Sunday, but I love to praise Jesus for all He has done in my life.

Spirit-filled people want to praise the Lord. I think sometimes we don't feel like praising. Life can be hard. It is easy to worship when everything in our lives is going well, but there are days when praise is a little more difficult. When we lose a job or a spouse tells us they don't want to stay in the marriage, when a loved one dies or we are wrongfully accused, those are hard days. I have certainly had hard days, but they should not prevent us from receiving the Holy Spirit. The hard days are some of the best days to show Jesus to a lost and hurting world. When people see us worshipping and praising God on our hard days, they take notice.

Let us open the Word of God and see what it shows us about praise.

Read all thirty-five verses of Genesis 29 to learn about Leah and her son Judah.

Who was Leah in relation to Jacob?

_____

Have you ever felt like Leah? Why or why not?

_____

_____

What would your response have been if you were put in that situation?

_____

_____

How many sons did Leah have before she gave birth to Judah?

_____

Does the Scripture say Jacob ever accepted Leah?

_____

What does the name Judah mean?

_____

Leah says in verse 35, "This time I will praise the LORD." The Hebrew word for *praise* used here is *yādâ*, and it literally means to "use (i.e. hold out) the hand; physically, to throw (a stone, an arrow) at or away; especially to revere or worship (with extended hands)."[1]

Leah learned to praise God no matter the circumstance. You can see that Leah felt rejected and not good enough by the names she chose for her first three sons. Scripture tells us in verses 31–33 that Leah was unloved, and in verse

34 she did not feel "attached" to Jacob. What Scripture does tell us is that Leah decided, "This time I will praise the LORD" (v. 35). After giving birth to three sons and hoping she would be loved and accepted by her husband, Leah *decided*.

Scripture does not tell us that Jacob ever loved and accepted Leah. All we read is that Leah praised the Lord. Was Leah blessed? If you follow the bloodline, you will see that Jesus is a direct descendant of Judah. (See Matthew 1:1–16.) What a blessing!

Now let's look at a New Testament example of praise. In Acts 16 Paul and Silas had been directed by the Holy Spirit to witness to people in Macedonia. Paul commanded a demon to leave a fortune teller, and that made the men who were making money from her very angry.

Read what happens next in Acts 16:20–34.

What did the chief magistrates do to Paul and Silas?

_____

_____

How would you feel if you were Paul?

_____

_____

What would your response have been?

_____

_____

How did Paul and Silas respond?

_____

_____

What happened because of Paul and Silas' response to their situation?

_____

_____

Praise is something we can choose to do despite our circumstances. No matter what is going on in our lives, we always have something to praise God for. There is an entire book in the Bible filled with praises, prayers, and songs: Psalms. Our heavenly Father wants us to come to Him with exactly what is on our hearts. As did David, the author of many psalms, and Leah and Paul, we will go through hard times in life, but for the Holy Spirit to be activated in our situation, we must praise.

What can we praise God for in our darkest moments? We can praise Him for what He has done for us in the past. We can praise God for what He is going to do to glorify Himself in and through us. We can praise God for what He is doing for us in our moment of challenge. There is *always* something to praise God for.

Sometimes we feel we can't get past the loss, disappointment, anxiety, depression, or negative emotion. We just need to praise our way through it. If you praise your way through the moment of crisis or challenge, it kills the enemy inside you, the enemy in front of you, and the enemy that binds you. Praise helps to turn our attention off ourselves and our situations and focus on the One who is in control of every situation. Our praise takes our focus from the darkness to the light. Our praise helps turn our hopelessness to the Giver of hope.

Read Psalm 42:5, 8, 11.

Where do we put our hope?

_____

_____

When we hope, what shall we do?

_____

_____

Our praise reminds our enemy that we have a much greater hope than our circumstances and feelings dictate. Our praise is our declaration that we have the power of the Holy Spirit in our lives, which enables us to overcome any situation we face. When we praise the Lord, our downcast souls are lifted, and we can lift our hands to our Maker and trust Him with everything! Our surrender is His victory, and our praise is our battle cry. Receive the Holy Spirit through praise and give God the glory for all He has done, is doing, and will do in your life!

DAY 5

UNITY

Behold, how good and how pleasant it is for
brethren to dwell together in unity!

—Psalm 133:1, kjv

Y**OU HAVE ALMOST** completed another week studying the Holy Spirit! I am so proud of your diligence and perseverance. Let's pause just for a minute and praise God for all He is doing in and through our lives:

God, we praise You today for who You are and thank You for all the ways You are revealing the goodness of Your heart to us. Thank You for teaching us to trust Your character and Your intentions. Thank You for giving us the Holy Spirit, who enables us to become all that You have called us to become, do all that You have called us to do, and see all that You would have us to see. Amen.

As we complete our week of learning how to *receive* the Holy Spirit, we cannot dismiss the fact that we are called to unity within the body of Christ. Throughout Scripture we are given examples of how God's children have struggled to be unified. We must read no further than Genesis to see how quickly man can turn on one another. Adam and Eve turned on each other in the Garden of Eden (Gen. 3). Cain turned on and killed his brother Abel (Gen. 4). There is also Jacob, who stole the birthright of his twin brother, Esau (Gen. 25), and Joseph, who was hated by his brothers and sold into slavery (Gen. 37). And we can't forget the half-brothers Ishmael and Isaac, whose descendants are still at war today. That is just in *Genesis*!

When we turn to the New Testament, we see that even some of Jesus' disciples had disagreements. (See Matthew 18:1, Mark 9:33–34, and Luke 22:23.) Just

because we read about struggles and people not getting along in Scripture does not mean the Holy Spirit does not want us to live in unity. The opposite is true.
Read John 17:20–23.

What did Jesus ask God for in verse 21?

_____

_____

Why did Jesus ask for this?

_____

_____

What relationship does our unity emulate?

_____

_____

What is at stake when we are not unified?

_____

_____

God calls us to live in unity with one another, just as the Godhead are in unity with one another. Jesus tells us this is very important, and when we get to the Book of Acts we see that unity is just as important as the Holy Spirit descends and the church begins to grow.
Read Acts 2:44–47.

What group of people were gathered together?

_____

What did their believing inspire them to do?

They continued daily with "one mind." In Greek this word is *homothymadon*. According to the *Outline of Biblical Usage*:

> A unique Greek word, used 10 of its 12 New Testament occurrences in the Book of Acts, helps us understand the uniqueness of the Christian community. Homothymadon is a compound of two words meaning to "rush along" and "in unison." The image is almost musical; a number of notes are sounded which, while different, harmonize in pitch and tone. As the instruments of a great concert under the direction of a concert master, so the Holy Spirit blends together the lives of members of Christ's church.[1]

Strong's defines this word as "unanimously: with one accord (mind)."[2] The word *homothymadon* leads us to understand that we are all part of the body of Christ, and we all have roles to play in fulfilling His purposes. We should not disagree and be divided, because disunity turns people away from the gospel. When we as followers of Jesus allow the Holy Spirit to help us live together in unity, we get to be a part of spreading the gospel, seeing signs and wonders and "having favor with all the people" as the Lord adds to our numbers daily those who are being saved (Acts 2:46–47).

There is a blessing that comes with unity not only in our homes but also in our churches. You can read through the Book of Acts and see that when the Holy Spirit was doing mighty works, believers had come together in unity. God is unlimited, His resources are unlimited, and His power is unlimited. I have seen Him provide in too many ways to count. I cannot help but wonder what the church would look like today if we came together in the unity of the Holy Spirit.

If the church stopped being divided over worship styles or the sizes of buildings, how many people would come to know Jesus and His saving grace? What if the church chose to come together to reach the world for His glory? What if the church did as the early believers did and sold their possessions to help advance the gospel? What if we decided to love those in our homes and put aside our selfish desires so our children would have a healthy example of how a relationship with God should be? I think we would experience the unlimited power of the Holy Spirit and that our homes, schools, workplaces, cities, counties, nation, and world could not deny Jesus.

Unity brings the blessing of God into our homes, our churches, our friendships, and our ministries. Unity is where God commands the blessing. Wouldn't you like to have the blessings of God in your life?

> Whom do you need to reach out to today to make a relationship right?

_____

_____

> What idea are you holding on to that the Holy Spirit may be asking you to lay down?

_____

_____

> Whom would you need to forgive for the Holy Spirit to be *unlimited* in your life?

_____

_____

> What gifts has God given you that you can use right now to help bring unity among believers?

_____

_____

Why not call someone you have had a disagreement with to make the relationship right? Why not let go of the idea of what we have "always done" to allow the Holy Spirit to do something new? Why not extend forgiveness for the sake of spreading God's love? Why don't we ask the Holy Spirit how to walk in unity with our brothers and sisters in Christ? Friend, let's look beyond our own selfish desires and ask the Holy Spirit what He desires for the advancement of the gospel. Let us look for ways to be unified so we can see the unlimited power of the Holy Spirit in our lives and in our churches!

> Therefore if there is any encouragement in Christ, if there is any consolation of love, if there is any fellowship of the Spirit, if any affection and compassion, make my joy complete by being of the same mind, maintaining the same love, united in spirit, intent on one purpose.
> —PHILIPPIANS 2:1–2, NASB

REST: EMPTY AND FILL

TAP INTO
GOD'S POWER
week3.unlimitedguide.info

WELCOME TO WEEK 3! Before we dive into this week's material, let's take a moment and praise God for the work He did in us over the last two weeks. Pray with me:

God, thank You for bringing us deeper into obedience and to the unity of Your Holy Spirit. As we grow in the grace of surrender, Your promises and Your power become even more evident to us and in us. We praise You for Your goodness and faithfulness to us, knowing that the work You have started in us, You will carry forward in us again this week. Amen.

I am sure of this, that he who began a good work in you will bring it to completion at the day of Jesus Christ.

—PHILIPPIANS 1:6

DAY 1
VESSELS

...put off your old self, which belongs to your former manner of life and is corrupt through deceitful desires, and to be renewed in the spirit of your minds.

—EPHESIANS 4:22–23

WE ARE CONTINUING to work through our acronym REST, and this week we are focusing on the *E*: empty and fill.

If we are going to look at emptying and filling, we need to know *what* we are emptying and filling. Let's take a minute to see what the Bible says about the "vessel" or the "temple" that contains the Holy Spirit.

What comes to mind when you hear the word *vessel*? I think of a couple things: blood vessels and ships. The Bible talks about vessels, but it is not talking about veins or ships. A vessel in Scripture was a household utensil that either held liquid for serving or was used to hold waste.

Read 2 Timothy 2:20.

What does this verse tell us vessels are made from?

What do the two different vessels represent according to this verse?

There were two different vessels used in biblical times. One of them was a vessel for clean water (honorable), used to serve guests, and it was made of gold and silver. Then there were vessels used for waste (dishonorable), and they were made of wood and earth or clay. It would have been a great dishonor to be a guest in someone's home and be served from the vessel used for waste. It was very important that the honorable vessels not be contaminated by the dishonorable.

In 2 Timothy, Paul uses a metaphor of vessels to refer to our bodies. Scripture tells us we are "vessels for the Holy Spirit."

Read 2 Timothy 2:22–26.

What is Paul saying the dishonorable vessel needs to get rid of?

_____

_____

Is your vessel a vessel of honor or dishonor? Why? What would you need to do to become an honorable vessel?

_____

_____

The sins of our flesh make us dishonorable vessels. If we flee from sin and follow God, then we become vessels of honor and are useful for serving the Lord.

Do you believe it is possible for you to be an honorable vessel? Why or why not?

_____

_____

We "all have sinned and fall short of the glory of God" (Rom. 3:23). First John 3:4 (NASB) tells us that "everyone who practices sin also practices lawlessness;

and sin is lawlessness," and the verse just before it says, "And everyone who has this hope fixed on Him purifies himself, just as He is pure" (1 John 3:3, NASB). We can be honorable vessels! With the help of the Holy Spirit, we no longer practice sin; we repent when the Holy Spirit convicts us, and by putting our trust in Jesus we become pure.

Being filled with the Holy Spirit is what makes it possible for us to be honorable vessels. However, each of us must participate in making our vessel a clean place for the Holy Spirit to reside. Warren W. Wiersbe put it this way: "For God to be able to use us as vessels, we must be empty, clean, and available. He will take us and fill us and use us for His glory. But if we are filled with sin or defiled by disobedience, He will first have to purge us; and that might not be an enjoyable experience."[1]

I love what Paul tells us in 2 Corinthians 4:7–10. Read that passage.

What do we have in our "jar of clay," or our vessel?

_____

_____

Whom does this belong to?

_____

_____

The term translated here as "surpassing power" or "surpassing greatness" is *hyperbolē*, and it means "a throwing beyond others...[as an adverb] preeminently: abundance, (far more) exceeding, excellency, more excellent, beyond (out of) measure."[2] The treasure in our vessels is exceedingly excellent, and it belongs to God, not to us. The Holy Spirit resides inside us, and the treasure is beyond anything we can imagine. How do I know this? Let's look at what the Bible says.

What dwells in us according to 1 Corinthians 3:16?

_____

_____

What dwells in us according to Romans 8:11?

_____

_____

The Holy Spirit lives in us, and with a treasure like that, shouldn't we want to have a vessel that is empty, clean, and available?

God tells us that we are filled with the Holy Spirit if we have put our faith in Jesus, but the issue with us remaining filled is that we are merely "fragile clay jars" (2 Cor. 4:7, NLT), which means we crack and leak easily.

Is your vessel broken? If so, what caused the break?

_____

_____

Do you struggle with pride, comfort, insecurities, or misperceptions? If so, name those things here—the areas where pride is present in your life, the insecurities and perceptions that hinder you.

_____

_____

What are some other things that make your life fractured or unclean?

_____

_____

_____

While we will look more into this later this week, I would like for you to begin praying that God will convict you of what is preventing your vessel from being "honorable" and give you a vision for what your life could look like if your vessel were clean. When we allow the Holy Spirit to repair our vessels, we make ourselves available to be used by God in a mighty way. That is something to celebrate!

TRANSFORMATION

Do not be conformed to this world, but be transformed by the renewal of your mind, that by testing you may discern what is the will of God, what is good and acceptable and perfect.

—ROMANS 12:2

L ET'S BEGIN TODAY by praying that the Holy Spirit will help us understand true transformation and that we will be able to receive what He shows us:

God, we are not capable of changing ourselves, and so often we cannot even imagine what change in our lives would look like. As the One who restores and makes all things new, give us a vision today for the ways You would transform us into Your image as we come to trust You and Your purposes for us more deeply. Amen.

Yesterday we talked about the fact that we are vessels for the Holy Spirit and why we need to be clean vessels so the Holy Spirit will not be quenched in our lives. Before we work on how to empty and fill our vessels with the Holy Spirit's unlimited resources, we need to talk about our minds. The mind is where change needs to happen first. Until you determine in your mind that change needs to happen, it is difficult to convince the rest of your body to comply. Our minds are so powerful. We have thought patterns that have been developed over our entire lives. We may have some memories that need to disappear but are difficult to shake. There may be some harsh words people have spoken to us that we cannot forget.

Our minds are a force to be reckoned with. Mentally we tend to get stuck in a rut. We have a hard time thinking about something new when our minds have been trained to think the same thing time after time. We have the same "stinking thinking" day after day, moment after moment, and don't do anything to change it—or we give up before our minds have been fully transformed.

Most of us believe that when we ask Jesus into our hearts, the hard work is over. Friend, once you ask Jesus into your heart, the hard work of transforming your mind *begins*. Why is it hard work? Because we are born in our flesh, and the enemy does not want us to have transformed minds. He works hard to keep us in a pit. Here is the hope: God did not leave us on our own. He sent us the Holy Spirit to live inside us and help create in us something new!

Read 2 Corinthians 5:17.

If any man is in who?

_____

_____

What is the man who is in that person?

_____

_____

What happens to the person who is in Christ?

_____

_____

The Greek word translated "he is a new" is *kainos*, meaning "of uncertain affinity; new (especially in freshness)."[1] I decided to look up the word *freshness* in the dictionary, and this is what I found: "having its original qualities unimpaired: such as (1) full of or renewed in vigor: refreshed; (2) not stale, sour, or decayed; (3) not faded; (4) not worn or rumpled...not salt (1) free from taint: pure; (2) of wind: moderately strong."[2] When we are in Christ, we are not stale, sour, or decayed. We are pure! One way to begin transforming our minds is to believe that we are made new, that we have a "freshness."

Have you ever considered that you were "made new"?
Does it change how you want to think?

_____

_____

How does this concept make you feel?

_____

_____

Let's look at a few more verses of Scripture. Read Ephesians 4:20–24.

In verse 22, what is Paul referencing?

_____

_____

What are we to do?

_____

_____

In verse 23, what are we to renew?

_____

_____

How are we to do that, according to verse 24?

_____

_____

What is our new self the likeness of? What are the attributes of that likeness?

_____

_____

I believe if you can understand that you are a "new creation in Christ," you can overcome your old thought patterns. Transforming our minds depends so much on whose we believe we are. Once we understand whose we are, we must learn what to think about.

Read Philippians 4:7–8.

List the things we should dwell on.

_____

_____

Think of something that leads you to a negative thought pattern. Write how you can transform that thought by applying Philippians 4:8.

_____

_____

This is how you begin transforming your mind. Brothers and sisters, again, our thoughts are so powerful. To renew your mind, make sure your thoughts align with Scripture. If you find yourself thinking something that doesn't align with Philippians 4:8, look for what the Scriptures say about the subject and repeat that verse(s) to yourself throughout the day. Memorizing Scripture is an important key to transforming our minds.

Since we are made new in Christ and the Holy Spirit dwells in us, we have the power to overcome our old thought patterns.

Read 1 Corinthians 2:12–16.

For those of us who have received Christ, what did we receive from God? As a result, what will we understand?

_____

_____

What does the Spirit interpret?

_____

_____

How can we understand the Lord's instruction?

_____

_____

Do you consider that good news? Why or why not?

_____

_____

_____

We have the mind of Christ through the Holy Spirit! We no longer think what we have always thought. We are made new, and so are our thoughts! When we think about things that are lovely, true, just, and praiseworthy, we are no longer living with our old thought patterns. We are rerouting our thoughts to align with the mind of Christ through the power of the Holy Spirit! For us to access all that the Holy Spirit has for us, we need to allow Him to help us transform our thoughts. Remember, the Holy Spirit is the Spirit of Truth, and as Jesus said in John 8:32, the truth will set you free!

DAY 3
EMPTY

But I say, walk by the Spirit, and you will
not gratify the desires of the flesh.
—GALATIANS 5:16

WELCOME BACK TO another day of learning how to be an honorable vessel for the Holy Spirit to do mighty works in and through! Let's pray that God will help us receive truth today and encourage us as we take a hard look at ourselves in order to become more like Christ:

God, we are so often full of the things we ought to be empty of and empty of the things we need to be full of. There is more clutter within us than we know how to name. Show us the things You are calling us to clear out to make space for the good work You are doing in us now. Amen.

The nineteenth-century evangelist D. L. Moody said, "Before we pray that God would fill us, I believe we ought to pray that He would empty us. There must be an emptying before there can be a filling; and when the heart is turned upside down, and everything that is contrary to God is turned out, then the Spirit will come."[1] There are things in your life that have secretly taken root and now influence your thoughts, words, and actions without you knowing.

Before the Holy Spirit can bring renewal, you must be willing to discard the selfish, sinful things that take up space in your heart. Some things have become so familiar that you may not even recognize them as sin or something to empty yourself of. Please open your eyes to see and your ears to hear what the Holy Spirit wants you to discover because He wants you to live in the fullness of His unlimited power and presence.

Does the thought of being "emptied" scare you at all? Why or why not?

_____

_____

How can your fears or hesitations keep you from experiencing the Holy Spirit moving in your life and leading you in a greater way?

_____

_____

Read Colossians 3:5, 8–9.

What did these verses reveal about what you need to empty yourself of? Write them here. *Please do not rush past this.*

_____

_____

_____

Does it seem possible to empty yourself of *all* these things? Why or why not?

_____

_____

In your flesh, this process will be impossible unless you rely on the Holy Spirit—because you don't even know the full extent of your internal clutter. Take a minute to pause and pray. Pray for the Holy Spirit to convict you. (I know this is hard, but remember that anything the Holy Spirit reveals will be for the sake of your own freedom!)

When you receive a fresh filling of the Holy Spirit and ask Him to convict you of sin, you must welcome His conviction of all areas that need improvement. This could change from one day to the next. Today it may be your attitude or your thoughts, words, or reactions that you realize are displeasing to God. Tomorrow it could be your emotions. You should consistently feel conviction until you have allowed the Holy Spirit to help you work through the issue.

Conviction will prompt you to repent and draw closer to God, but guilt will always provoke a brokenness that pushes you further from God. An opinion is something you hold, but conviction is something that holds you. With that in mind, read Colossians 3:5, 8–9 again.

> Did the Holy Spirit reveal anything new to you the second time you read this passage? If so, what was it?

_____

_____

Let's look at another scripture to see if there are other things we should empty from our vessels so the Holy Spirit can move freely in our lives. I am not doing this to torture you, I promise. I want you to have complete liberty so you can experience the unlimited power of the Holy Spirit.

Read Galatians 5:19–26.

> List what we should rid ourselves of according to these verses.

_____

_____

According to these verses, by what power can we rid ourselves of the deeds of the flesh?

_____

_____

Again, I know this is a hard exercise, but if we do the hard work to see what sin we have in our lives, the Holy Spirit will help us overcome those challenges so we can reflect Jesus by the power of the Holy Spirit. I also want to make sure we understand that we *all* sin—daily. If the treasure of the Holy Spirit is in us and we allow Him full access to our vessel, He will convict us of that sin, and we will seek forgiveness and change our ways; by doing this, we maximize the unlimited power of the Holy Spirit in our lives.

We need to make sure we are not practicing sin. Read 1 John 3:8–10. The Greek word translated "practice" in these verses is *poieō*. It means to "abide, agree, appoint, avenge, band together...execute, exercise...gain, give, have, hold, journeying...perform, provide."[2] Now read 1 John 3:8–10 again, applying this definition to the passage.

Those who "band together, execute, exercise, hold, journey" with sin align with whom?

_____

_____

Those who "band together, execute, exercise, hold, journey" with righteousness align with whom?

_____

_____

Practicing sin is much different from sinning. Practicing sin means we willfully stay in sin and keep going back to it, choosing our flesh over the

Spirit day after day. First John 1:8 tells us, "If we say we have no sin, we deceive ourselves, and the truth is not in us." We all inevitably sin, but we put ourselves in alignment with our enemy when we "practice" sin, and the Holy Spirit cannot reside where the enemy is at work.

I am about to ask you a hard question:

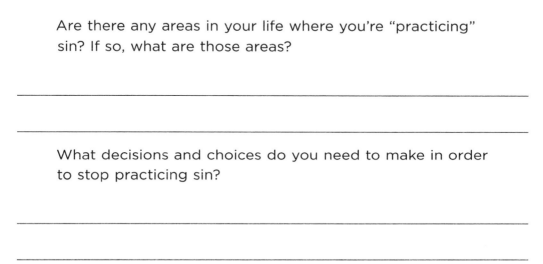

> Are there any areas in your life where you're "practicing" sin? If so, what are those areas?
>
> _____
>
> _____
>
> What decisions and choices do you need to make in order to stop practicing sin?
>
> _____
>
> _____

If you are practicing sin, you need to ask someone on staff at your church who they recommend you speak with so they can pray for you and hold you accountable.

Friend, the Holy Spirit wants us to pursue righteousness and surrender our lives to Him alone. He loves us and wants His best for us, but if we hold on to the things we need to rid ourselves of, we cannot live the abundant life to which we are called.

I want you to see that God is so very good to us! He had a plan from the beginning, and it was to redeem us from our sins through His Son, Jesus. After Jesus lived a perfect life and gave Himself up for us as a sacrifice for our sins, He sent His Holy Spirit in unlimited supply so we could live out His personal plan for our lives as we yield to Him!

If we can ask the Holy Spirit to help us empty ourselves of the "deeds of the flesh" by convicting us and showing us ourselves through the lens of truth (which is the Word of God), then the fruit of the Spirit will be evident in our lives—in unlimited quantity!

Before we can fill our vessels with the treasure of the Holy Spirit, we must empty ourselves of our fleshly desires. This can only be done by allowing the Holy Spirit access to those places that we hope no one sees. Once you are emptied of your fleshly desires and filled with the Holy Spirit, there can be no question of who gets the glory for all the wonderful things that flow from your life.

Good work today. That was hard. I am so proud of you!

DAY 4
FILL

Seek the LORD and his strength; seek his presence continually!
—PSALM 105:4

I AM SO GLAD you are back with me today. Congratulations on working through the tough work yesterday. You will be blessed for the work you are doing.

Let's take a moment to ask the Lord to fill us with the Holy Spirit and encourage us in this journey.

God, as You have taken us through the painful process of emptying ourselves, we are now craving to be full of all that You have for us. As You have guided us faithfully to pour out the things within us that have only hindered and harmed us, we ask that You pour Your Spirit, truth, and wisdom into us today. Amen.

This week we have been continuing in our REST acronym. On day 1 we began by talking about our vessels, and we learned that vessels are used for emptying and filling. Our goal in working through this study is to have the Holy Spirit alive and active in our lives so God's glory will be revealed and others will come to know Jesus. For us to have the Holy Spirit moving in our lives, we must be filled with Him!

Read Ephesians 5:18.

What are we to be filled with?

_____

What two behaviors are contrasted in this verse?

_____

Paul contrasts being "drunk with wine" with being "filled with the Spirit." Being drunk with wine causes us to lose control and leaves us with guilt and shame. Being filled with the Spirit causes us to have self-control that brings lasting joy and glorifies God. If we are going to serve God effectively and be available to pour into others, we need His power constantly—and that takes a regular filling of the Holy Spirit.

You might think, "Benny, if the Holy Spirit came to live inside me when I believed Jesus died for my sins, what is the difference between being baptized in the Holy Spirit and being filled with the Holy Spirit?" That is a great question. The baptism in the Spirit means you belong to the body of Christ and to Him. The baptism makes us one in the body of Christ.

Read Ephesians 4:3–6.

What are we to be diligent to preserve?

_____

How many times is the word *one* written in these passages?

_____

_____

How many times is the word *all* written in these passages?

_____

_____

What is Paul, the author of Ephesians, trying to convince us of?

_____

_____

The Holy Spirit's work in the body of Christ is revealed in unity. There is nothing worse than a church full of half-filled people. A church full of Spirit-filled people will turn the world upside down for the glory of God! That is what it is to be baptized in the Holy Spirit.

When we are filled with the Holy Spirit, we realize the power we have, and we are made effective witnesses for the kingdom. Look at Ephesians 5:18 again.

God looked at people like us and told us to be filled with the Spirit—to invite the very presence of God to live inside us in the form of His Spirit. That is incredible!

"Be filled with the Spirit" is both a personal command and a plural command, meaning that as believers we are *all* to be filled with the Holy Spirit. In the original text the reader would understand that the verb "filled" is in the present tense and reads closer to "keep on being filled." And as often happens in the Bible, this verb is also passive, meaning we do not fill ourselves; we allow the Holy Spirit access to fill us. This means we are controlled by the Holy Spirit in our mind, emotions, and will.

With all this in mind,

> Read Ephesians 5:18 again and write what this verse is telling you.

_____

_____

This is what I wrote: "And do not do anything that causes you to act out of control that leaves you feeling ashamed or guilty. Instead, if you are a believer of Jesus Christ—all of you—keep on allowing the Holy Spirit access for continual filling and be controlled in your mind, in your emotions, and in your will."

Now read Acts 4:31.

> What were the followers doing?

_____

What happened while they were praying?

_____

Who was filled? Was it just one or two people?

_____

What were they able to do after they were filled?

_____

The word translated "filled" in Acts 4:31 is *pimplēmi*, and it means "to 'fill' (literally or figuratively (imbue, influence, supply)); specially, to fulfill... accomplish, full...furnish."[1] All the followers that were together praying were filled, accomplished, full, furnished with the Holy Spirit. If you go on to read further in Acts 2, you will see that the followers were *one*, and they openly shared what they had.

Read Acts 4:33.

What were the apostles able to do?

_____

_____

How were they able to do those things?

_____

_____

The word *power* in this verse is *dynamis*, "force; specially, miraculous power... ability, abundance...mighty (wonderful) work."[2] Brothers and sisters, we all have access to this same power. How exciting would it be if the church at large had empty vessels and the Holy Spirit filled us to overflowing so that we were boldly "giving witness to the resurrection of the Lord Jesus" and there was "abundant grace" upon us all? Can you imagine it? We will talk about ways to access this filling, but today I would like to talk about how often we need to be filled, and why.

How often do you think you need to be filled with the Holy Spirit? Why?

_____

_____

Have you ever tried doing something God has called you to do without being filled with the Holy Spirit? If so, how did you feel?

_____

_____

Have you tried to be a good spouse or parent or to serve others without a fresh filling of the Holy Spirit? If so, how did that go?

_____

_____

Are you open to allowing the Holy Spirit to work in and through you? If so, take a moment to write that desire in your own words in the form of a short prayer.

_____

_____

There is one more thing we need to remember: we must be open to being filled. What good is a vessel that leaks and yet has a lid that won't come off?

If we are vessels that house the Holy Spirit, we can limit the power of the Holy Spirit in us! We put a lid on. If we are open vessels, we can contain that which is bigger than us. If we are open vessels, we can discern what we don't already know. If we are open vessels, we are open to more truth. If we are open vessels, we have access to the always flowing living water and all the things that have eternal value. If we are open vessels and remain open—keeping our hearts, minds, and lives open to the things the Holy Spirit has for us—the outpouring of the Holy Spirit becomes unlimited!

Here is what I know: Without a fresh filling of the Holy Spirit's power daily and remaining open, you will feel drained and depleted. If you get up in the morning and interact with anyone that day, you need the filling of the Holy Spirit. Before I go into a meeting or a conversation with anyone, I ask God to fill me with the Holy Spirit so I will not speak from my flesh. (See Ephesians 5:18–21.) We are *all* sinners (Rom. 3:23). That means our vessels leak, and we need to sit under a faucet with our lid removed and allow God to fill us daily— some days second by second. As Billy Sunday once explained, "The only way to keep a broken vessel full is to keep it always under the tap."[3]

We need to go to the well of living water daily to be filled to overflowing so we have something to give those in need. We need to be filled daily so we can be patient, kind, and loving to others. We need to be filled daily so we can have joy in times of sorrow and so the world can see peace in us. We need to be filled daily to be kind to those who are not so kind to us and gentle to those who are not so gentle. (See Ephesians 5:20–21.) We need to be filled with the Holy Spirit so a broken, lost, and fearful world will want to know the One who fills you and me daily.

The Spirit was sent to empower and fill us with unlimited power. It is our job to allow Him to work in and through us. Knowing Him and surrendering to Him allows you to live fully by a power (*dynamis*) greater than yourself. In my experience, when you choose to be continually filled by the Holy Spirit, you will live out the most exciting journey you could ever imagine! He will call you higher, take you further, and provide more abundantly than all you can ask or think! Go to the well, drink daily, and be filled to overflowing!

DAY 5
POUR

May the God of hope fill you with all joy and peace in believing, so that by the power of the Holy Spirit you may abound in hope.
—ROMANS 15:13

PRAY THAT YOU were inspired yesterday to allow the Holy Spirit to access your life! There is so much joy in obeying God and allowing His Spirit to fill you to capacity!

Let's take a moment to praise God for all the blessings in our lives. Let's praise Him for being the Creator of all things and in control of everything!

God, thank You for being the One who fills us. You do not just fill us once, but You continue to fill, renew, and refresh us over and over. Thank You for being the well that never runs dry. Thank You for always having enough, for always being enough. As You continue to fill and refill us, show us what to do with what we have been given so the work You are doing in us can be a resource for a thirsty world around us. Amen.

We have discussed so much this week. We have talked about what being a vessel means in relation to receiving the Holy Spirit. We have seen that our minds need to be transformed so our vessels can hold His presence and that we need to empty our vessels of our flesh to make room for the unlimited power of the Holy Spirit. Yesterday we discussed that our vessels need to be filled. Today we will talk about what the outpouring of the Holy Spirit should look like.

I want you to know that just as I was not the pastor, husband, father, friend, or relative five years ago that I am today, I pray that I am not the same man five years from today. The overflowing power of the Holy Spirit changes us over time as we spend time reading God's Word, praying, and obeying His promptings.

As we give the Holy Spirit unlimited access in our lives, we become better at allowing the fruit of the Holy Spirit to be in abundant supply so we have what we need to give others as we interact with them. May we all get better each day, and may others be able to see that we have spent time with Jesus.

Read Galatians 5:22–23.

> What "fruit" do we bear as we live by the Spirit, according to these verses?

_____

_____

> Which ones of these do you have an abundance of most days?

_____

_____

> Which ones do you feel like you need more of?

_____

_____

These verses talk about the fruit of the Spirit, and this should be evidence of the Holy Spirit's activity in our lives. When we received the Holy Spirit, we received all the fruit. We just allow our flesh to keep us from bearing the fruit of the Spirit—and we need to continually work on that. When we allow the Holy Spirit's presence and power to change us from the inside out, we begin to look more like Christ—and that is the goal!

Read Acts 4:13.

> How did the council see Peter and John?

_____

The council recognized Peter and John as having been with whom?

_____

_____

Do you feel ordinary? What makes you feel this way?

_____

_____

Do you feel like you are not trained in the Scriptures? Do you feel disqualified from leading others into a relationship with Jesus? Why or why not?

_____

_____

How does this verse encourage you?

_____

_____

When I first came to Christ, I didn't know anything about church or religion or how to lead others to Jesus. I didn't know anything about the Bible either! All I knew was that I was no longer the same. I was different. Things that never bothered me before bothered me. I was convicted about things I never thought were wrong before. There was a change in me, and I now recognize that change was the Holy Spirit in me no longer being able to live with the old me. I was a new creation. I will tell you, with the power of the Holy Spirit I have grown into who I am today (not perfect, just different than I was)—and the unlimited power of the Holy Spirit can do that for you too!

Read Galatians 5:22–23 again.

This is how we are to live with *everybody*. Love, joy, peace, patience, kindness, goodness, faithfulness, gentleness, and self-control are what should flow from your vessel. The fruit of the Spirit is how we display Jesus to the world. So many people experience the opposite of this fruit that when we demonstrate just *one*, they often do not know how to respond.

Notice in verse 22 that the word *fruit* is singular. That is because there is only one Holy Spirit. We all need the Holy Spirit because we all need love, joy, peace, patience, kindness, goodness, long-suffering, and self-control. The Holy Spirit provides us with everything we need in every interaction of every day. God longs to see His people bearing the fruit of His Spirit.

Read Matthew 7:16–20.

How will you know someone is a follower of Jesus?

_____

_____

What does a good tree produce?

_____

What does Galatians 5:22–23 say a good fruit tree bears?

_____

_____

Write Matthew 7:20.

_____

_____

People outside the church should be able to point out a follower of Jesus based on how we treat others. We should look, speak, and behave differently than the rest of the world. We have the Holy Spirit living in us, and that means we should treat others differently.

Look up John 15:5 and write it down.

_____

_____

If we abide in Jesus, what happens?

_____

What can we do apart from Jesus?

_____

From the moment that you accept Jesus into your life, you have the Holy Spirit living inside you—which means the good fruit immediately begins to develop. That means *all* the fruit listed in Galatians 5:22–23 begins to develop. You should begin having more patience with others. You should begin loving those who are hard to love. You should be gentler and have more self-control. You won't suddenly wake up perfect, but you should see signs that the fruit of the Spirit is developing.

What fruit have you seen develop since you came to know the Lord?

_____

What fruit could use more cultivating (as you spend time abiding with Jesus)?

_____

How can you spend more time with Jesus today?

_____

_____

Who would benefit most from you spending time in God's Word? Are they worth the time?

_____

_____

When the Holy Spirit transforms your life from the inside out, the fruit of the Spirit will be evident to everyone you encounter. It becomes who you are and what you do without even trying. When you spend time with the Father, you will produce good fruit.

I pray you won't settle for just asking Jesus into your life. I pray you will choose to abide in Him and allow the Holy Spirit an all-access pass so you can live an abundant life that multiplies and maximizes the fruit of the Spirit. When you are multiplying and maximizing the fruit of the Holy Spirit, you will impact others for eternity—and that is worth everything. After all, that is what Jesus did for each of us!

REST: STUDY SCRIPTURE AND PRAY

TAP INTO GOD'S POWER
week4.unlimitedguide.info

AS WE JOURNEY deeper into the things God has called us to be filled with by focusing on the importance of Scripture and prayer, let's bow our heads together and pray:

God, I pray that You would speak to me and through me. I believe in the power of the Holy Spirit. Today I pray that You will speak to my heart and that the word You give me today will be a word in season. For all You do, I praise You! Amen.

DAY 1
DAILY BREAD

Oh how I love your law! It is my meditation all the day.
—PSALM 119:97

I AM SO GLAD you are back for week 4. Your time spent in God's Word will not return void!

This week we move to the third letter of our acronym REST, *S*, which reminds us to study Scripture and pray to activate the Holy Spirit in our lives. You may wonder which I think is more important, prayer or Bible study. I will tell you they are *both* important. Yet I find myself going to Scripture first every day because I want to hear what God needs to say to me before I start telling Him what I need from Him.

Many of us go to Scripture looking for answers to our questions and challenges. We want it to provide a quick fix for our struggles. God's Word is more than a fix-it guide. It is God's expression of love to us, and it directs us to Jesus. Scripture is not about us at all. With the Holy Spirit's help we can discover God's deep love for us in Scripture. By reading God's Word and seeing it as God's expression of His love for us, we discover God's will for our lives through the power of the Holy Spirit. That perspective deepens our desire to seek God's Word daily.

With that in mind, let's see what the Bible says about our need to study Scripture and to pray.

Read Matthew 6:9–14 and answer the following questions based on verse 11.

What does Jesus tell us to ask for?

How often are we to ask?

_____

_____

Why did Jesus teach us to ask for daily bread?

_____

_____

Let us now go to the Old Testament to see when God first supplied "bread" for His people. Read Exodus 16:1–15.

Where were the Israelites?

_____

Why were they grumbling?

_____

Who provided for them, and what did He provide?

_____

How long did His provision last?

_____

Read John 6:1–13.

What miracle did Jesus perform in this passage?

_____

What need was met for the multitude?

_____

In verse 12, what was the condition of the crowd?

_____

Now read John 6:30–36.

What was the crowd asking for this time?

_____

What story did they quote from their past?

_____

Write John 6:32–33 here.

_____

_____

Who gives the "true bread from heaven"?

_____

Read Mark 14:22 and write it here.

_____

_____

Underline the item Jesus offered before He spoke.

Now read John 6:57–58.

What came down from heaven?

_____

_____

How was this bread different from the bread in Exodus 16?

_____

_____

What do you understand Matthew 6:11 to mean now?

_____

_____

Does your understanding of Matthew 6:11 differ from when you first read it today? If so, how?

_____

_____

Jesus is showing us by example that we need to go to God daily and seek His provision. He is the Bread of Life. We need to have faith that He will provide for us. He provided for His people daily in the Old and New Testaments, and He will provide for us daily now.

Just as the Israelites needed to pick up the manna daily while they were in the desert, we must go to God's Word and pick up truth to be spiritually nourished daily. When we are spiritually nourished, the Holy Spirit empowers us to receive from God's Word and apply it in our lives, so we are living in His fullness. The Lord is not limiting you by only providing you with enough for the present day. It's quite the opposite. When you rely on Him to provide everything you need, He will make sure you live out of His abundance every day of your life. His provisions are unlimited!

BENEFITS OF STUDYING SCRIPTURE

But he answered, "It is written, 'Man shall not live by bread alone, but by every word that comes from the mouth of God.'"
—MATTHEW 4:4

BEFORE WE GO into the material today, let's take a few moments to praise God for His Word and for making it available to us. Let's praise Him for revealing Himself to us through Scripture:

God, we thank You for giving us Your Word, which feeds, nourishes, and sustains us. You do not let Your seed beg for bread—but we do ask for it, knowing that You love to give good gifts to Your children and that You delight when we feast on You in our hearts by faith. So, we come to Your table again, both humble and hungry. Amen.

Yesterday we learned that to keep the Holy Spirit active in our lives, we need to read and study God's Word daily. A lot of Christians use the Bible like a car manual, only pulling it out to read certain sections when there is a problem. But God didn't give us the Bible to increase our knowledge; He gave us the Bible to change our lives. How does it change our lives? Let's look in the Word of God to see some of its benefits.

Look up Romans 15:4 and write it here.

_____

_____

Why was Scripture written?

_____

_____

What might we have through the encouragement of Scripture?

_____

_____

Hope. In Greek the word is *elpis*, meaning "to anticipate, usually with pleasure...expectation or confidence."[1] Do you need hope today? Reading Scripture encourages us and gives us hope in every circumstance. The Holy Spirit will use Scripture to help us persevere in hard circumstances.

The first part of Romans 15:4 reminds us that the Word is also for our instruction. D. L. Moody said, "The Scriptures were not given to increase our knowledge, but to change our lives."[2] If we spend time in God's Word every day, our lives will change. We will find hope in hopeless situations, wisdom beyond our capacity, and instruction when we do not know what to do.

Now read Colossians 3:16.

What should dwell in you richly?

_____

_____

What will the Word of Christ in you cause you to do?

_____

_____

I would like to take a moment and look at the word *dwell* as it is used in Colossians 3:16. The Greek term is *enoikeō*, and it is derived from the word *oikeō*, meaning "to occupy a house, i.e. reside; by implication, to cohabit."[3] It means to feel at home. Paul tells us here to let the "word of Christ" feel at home so that when we are teaching, correcting, or worshipping, we are doing so with a heart of gratitude to God. I travel some, and I can tell you my favorite place to be is home. Home is where I am most comfortable. It is where I can be totally myself. Home is where I feel safe.

What are other benefits of God's Word dwelling in us? It gives us what we need in order to teach, to correct, and to worship the Lord, and it is the only offensive weapon we are given against our enemy.

Read Ephesians 6:11–17.

> Whom are we able to stand firm against when we put on the armor of God?

_____

_____

We have an enemy that wants to kill, steal, and destroy anything good in your life. Our enemy wants our marriages, families, children, and jobs to fail. Our enemy wants to make sure that if God is doing anything good in our lives, it is destroyed.

> Read verse 17 again and write it here.

_____

_____

> What is the sword of the Spirit?

_____

Jesus shows us the perfect example of how to use the sword of the Spirit to stand firm against the enemy. Read Matthew 4:1–11.

Who was Jesus led by?

_____

_____

How long had Jesus been fasting?

_____

_____

What did Jesus command Satan to do in verse 10?

_____

_____

How did Jesus refute the temptation of the enemy?

_____

_____

Read Deuteronomy 8:3; then Deuteronomy 6, verses 16 and 13, in that order.

In a traditional Jewish education boys would have memorized the first five books of the Bible (known as the Torah) by age ten. Because Jesus was raised in a traditional Jewish culture and studied in the synagogue as a child, He knew Scripture by memory and was able to apply biblical truth to specific situations. For every specific temptation Jesus faced when He was tempted by the devil in Matthew 4, He had precise Scripture to quote in response. If Jesus needed to rely on memorizing Scripture to escape temptation, so should we. The Bible is full of passages that can help us in times of temptation and suffering. If we have

Scripture memorized, the Holy Spirit can bring these passages to our remembrance when we need them most.

The Holy Spirit opens our minds to understand the Scriptures. In Acts 1:20 Peter quoted Psalm 69:25 and Psalm 109:8. His audience (the Jewish followers of Jesus) believed in the divine inspiration of the Old Testament and that the Scriptures could be applied to their situation.

Read 2 Timothy 3:16–17.

Whom is Scripture inspired by?

How much of Scripture is inspired?

How much Scripture is profitable?

All Scripture is God-breathed. In week 1 of this study guide we talked about the *ruach* of God. This is the same word used in this passage. The same breath God used to give Adam life inspired His Word. All sixty-six books, 1,189 chapters, and 31,102 verses of Scripture—every single word—is breathed by God! Because it is all breathed by God, all Scripture is profitable "for teaching, for reproof, for correction, and for training in righteousness" so that we may "be complete, equipped for every good work" (2 Tim. 3:16–17)!

Do you feel equipped for every good work? Why or why not?

If you do not feel equipped, then do not wait one more second to begin getting in God's Word daily. The Holy Spirit will never lead you in a way that is contradictory to God's Word, so when you spend time there, the Holy Spirit can guide and equip you.

Take some time to find a verse that would help you in your daily life right now. Write it down and put it in a place where you can see it regularly. You will find that after a few days you will have it memorized, and the Holy Spirit will bring it to your memory when you need it. You may hear yourself using that scripture as you pray for someone. That is the unlimited power of the Holy Spirit at work.

We study God's Word because as we do, the Holy Spirit uses its content to renew our minds and equip us for every good work. By reading God's Word daily and putting it to use, we gain hope, encouragement, and an offensive weapon in the face of our enemy. When the Word of God dwells in us, the Holy Spirit makes Himself at home, and at home with the Spirit is where we are safe! Let the Scripture be at home in you and bring life!

DAY 3
HOW TO PRAY

The prayer of a righteous person has great power as it is working.
—JAMES 5:16

YOU HAVE BEEN doing some really good work this week. I am so proud of you! Let us begin today by asking God to give us wisdom to understand His Word and the strength to obey what He is telling us:

God, we do not know how to pray as we ought. So, like Your disciples, we come to You in need, asking You to teach us. Thank You for not only answering us in prayer but also giving us the very questions to ask. Amen.

Scottish writer Robert Law once said, "Prayer is a mighty instrument, not for getting man's will done in heaven, but for getting God's will done on earth."[1]

Prayer is so important, and many of us do not use it as we should. We like to use it when we are in a crisis or when we *really* want something. Some of us use it to spread gossip or bring attention to what we are going through when we want sympathy. I am not saying we should not share prayer requests and pray for one another; I am just saying that God sees our hearts, and His intention is that we use prayer to develop an intimate relationship with Him.

Some of us have gone to God in prayer and felt like He did not answer (or didn't answer the way we expected), and we refuse to ask Him again because we think He is not listening or does not care. That is hard. I have learned that we often do things that feel good or seem right, but the best thing we can do is see what the Bible says. So, let's begin today by seeing what the Bible has to say about prayer.

Look up 1 Thessalonians 5:16–18 and write it here.

_____

_____

How are we to pray?

_____

_____

What does "without ceasing" mean to you?

_____

_____

Does that seem unattainable? Why or why not?

_____

_____

This verse tells me that we are to invite the Holy Spirit to be part of every task, every conversation, and every decision. British evangelist Smith Wigglesworth once said, "I don't often spend more than half an hour in prayer at one time, but I never go more than half an hour without praying."[2] That may mean you say a quick prayer for safety while driving. Before going into a meeting, I often say a quick prayer: "Lord, help me to say the right stuff, and nudge me when I've said enough." You can know the Holy Spirit better and fan the flame of His presence in your life through prayer. It is through Bible study and prayer that the Holy Spirit can influence our minds, hearts, and will.

I think Jesus is the best example to follow. We are told at least thirty-eight times in the Gospels (Matthew, Mark, Luke, and John) that Jesus was praying or went away to pray. He prayed often enough that His disciples asked Him to teach them how to pray.

Read Luke 11:1–4. You may have grown up saying the Lord's Prayer in church. If it is familiar to you, read this passage again slowly, asking the Holy Spirit to help you see it anew.

Did anything stick out to you? If so, what was it?

_____

_____

What aspect of this prayer has been hardest for you to understand?

_____

_____

I love that Jesus begins His prayer with "Our Father." I grew up not knowing my biological father, and my stepfather never let me forget that I was not biologically his. I never got to call my stepfather "Daddy" and always wanted to, so calling God "Father" means a lot to me. What Jesus does in Luke 11:1 is invite each of us into that Father-child relationship by using the pronoun *our*. It does not matter what your relationship with your earthly father is like; your heavenly Father loves you, and He wants you to approach Him feeling safe and loved. He is a good, good Father.

The Lord's Prayer goes on to remind us that our Father is in heaven and in control of *all* things. His name is to be "hallowed," as the King James Version puts it, meaning it should be honored, valued, treasured, esteemed, revered, and loved. We are to ask our Father to help us obey His commands joyfully here on earth as His will is done in heaven. In this, Jesus is teaching us to align our hearts with God's will for His kingdom before we ask Him to meet our daily needs and forgive our sins.

Do you feel your life pulling you out of alignment with God's plan? If so, how?

_____

_____

How would you need to align your prayer life?

_____

_____

Do you need to change your approach to prayer? If so, how?

_____

_____

This prayer is so deep and rich that I would encourage you to ask the Holy Spirit to continually open your eyes to how He would want you to apply it to your life. The Holy Spirit is truth, and He will guide you into all truth. He wants His kingdom, will, and glory to be expressed through our lives, and He does that in greater measure as we activate His power through our prayers.

There are more than 650 prayers and approximately 450 recorded answers to prayer in the Bible. In fact, prayer is mentioned in almost every chapter of the Book of Acts. God wants us to pray. He wants to involve us in what He is doing here on earth, so He gives us prayer as a way of forming a deep, personal relationship with Him. Relationships are built and sustained by constant communication, and prayer is our way of communicating with our heavenly Father. Of course God already knows every detail in our lives, but He likes being invited in. I have said it before, but it is worth mentioning again—the Holy Spirit is a gentleman.

Let's take a deeper dive into what Jesus is inviting us to do by looking at the example Christ set for us in the Garden of Gethsemane.

Read Matthew 26:36–44.

How do you think you would have responded to Jesus asking you to pray?

_____

_____

Do you think Peter and the two sons of Zebedee (James and John) knew what was coming next? Why or why not?

_____

_____

How would knowing what was going to happen change how you would pray?

_____

_____

Jesus asked three of the disciples to go farther into the garden with Him to pray. Look closely at verse 39. What did Jesus do?

_____

_____

Jesus went farther still to pray, praying to the point of bleeding from His brow. Has it ever seemed like Jesus was asking you to go farther with Him than He has asked others in your life? How did you respond?

_____

_____

Did you know what was ahead of you when you went farther with Jesus?

I will tell you that when God has called me to do things He has not asked of others around me, I have had *no idea* what was ahead of me!

In my years of serving the Lord I have learned that when God calls me to go deeper with Him, I need to try to stay awake and pray so I'll know what steps to take. Yet often my "spirit indeed is willing, but the flesh is weak" (Matt. 26:41), and all I have is the Word of the Lord and the Holy Spirit to guide me. Fortunately Romans 8:26 says, "Likewise the Spirit helps us in our weakness. For we do not know what to pray for as we ought, but the Spirit himself intercedes for us with groanings too deep for words."

How consistent is your prayer life?

Do you share with God all the details of your life, or do you think, "He already knows, so why repeat it?"

Do you think you are not worthy to go to God in prayer? If so, why?

Read Matthew 26:50.

What did Jesus call Judas in this scripture?

He calls you a friend too. Prayer is about building a relationship with God, and not one of us is too far gone to be invited in. Jesus always wants to take you further with Him and lead you to share in His suffering. He wants to take you to a place of complete trust and faith in what He is doing in and through you. That place of complete surrender is where God is glorified.

In the moments when we don't know what to pray, the Spirit takes over. Prayer builds our faith and allows us to have a rich relationship with our Creator and Father in heaven. We will look at the benefits of prayer tomorrow. For now, I encourage you to simply give God the details of your life in prayer and let the Holy Spirit minister to your soul.

DAY 4
BENEFITS OF PRAYER

But you, beloved, building yourselves up in your most
holy faith and praying in the Holy Spirit.
—JUDE 20

AS WE CONTINUE to work through our acronym REST—specifically focusing this week on our need to *study Scripture and pray*—let's ask our heavenly Father to be with us and teach us something new so we can have a more intimate relationship with Him and reveal His glory here on earth:

God, we know that You want to give only good gifts to Your children. As we come to You as children now, we are eager to open the good gifts You have prepared for us. Let us open them now in faith as You teach us the depths of this life of prayer to which we are called. Amen.

I have seen so many benefits of prayer in my life. My wife, Barbara, used to have multiple seizures every day, and we were told there was nothing the doctors could do. We prayed, and I am here to tell you she does not have any seizures today—she is healed! We wanted a child, and we were not able to conceive. We prayed, and God blessed us to adopt Savannah Abigail. I was told that Milner, Georgia, was too small for us to build a large church there. God has seen to it that we have around six thousand people attend most weekends. Glory, hallelujah! You cannot tell me God does not answer prayer. My life is full of examples of the benefits of praying.

Yesterday we saw that Jesus prayed often and gave us an outline for how to pray. Today I want us to look at several benefits of prayer.

As I mentioned previously, God has answered so many of my prayers. What He has done for me, He will do for you. When we pray, God listens. Look at what the Bible says.

Look up Psalm 17:6 and write it here.

_____

_____

Now read Psalm 116:1–2.

What does God hear?

_____

_____

How does He hear?

_____

_____

Do you feel like God does not hear you when you pray? If so, why do you feel that way?

_____

_____

_____

Friend, God hears you. Psalm 116:2 says He has "inclined his ear to me." To incline one's ear is to really focus on what is being said; to be engaged.

Read Isaiah 65:24.

What does God tell us in this verse?

_____

_____

Sometimes God answers our prayers and says, "Go!" Sometimes He says, "No!" Sometimes He says, "Slow," because the timing is not right. And sometimes He says, "Grow!" because we are not yet in the right place with Him. What I know is that He "inclines his ear to me."

The psalmist was writing from a place of deep sorrow. If you were to read more of Psalm 116 you would see statements like, "I suffered distress and anguish"; "I am greatly afflicted"; and "All mankind are liars" (vv. 3, 10–11). He is calling on the name of the Lord, trusting that God inclines His ear and will respond to his pleas.

> When you call out to God, do you trust that He hears you? Why or why not?

_____

_____

> What prayers have you prayed that God has answered?

_____

_____

_____

Our Father wants to give good gifts to us. Read Matthew 7:11.

> If you have children, do you like to give good gifts to them? What is a good gift for your child?

_____

_____

If you do not have children, do you like to give good gifts to friends or loved ones? If so, what is a good gift?

_____

God wants to give us gifts that are beneficial, good, valuable, and virtuous. If He has not answered a prayer, He has something better in mind for you. It is not that He has turned away from you or is punishing you. He just wants what is beneficial, good, valuable, and virtuous for *you*! Trust Him! He is a good, good Father. He loves you, and He is near when we pray.

Look up Psalm 145:18 and write it here.

_____

_____

The Lord is near to whom?

_____

How must we call upon Him?

_____

We must call upon God "in truth." Another word used here is *integrity*, and it translates as "faith." We have a responsibility when we pray to make sure our vessels are clean (refer to week 3, day 3) so the Holy Spirit is not quenched and can hear us.

Read Psalm 66:18.

What happens if I "regard wickedness in my heart" (NASB)?

_____

_____

If we approve of wickedness (sin) and have ongoing sin in our lives, then the Lord will not hear us when we pray to Him. He wants to hear us, He desires to have a relationship with us, and He wants to walk with us every step of every day. But when we "regard wickedness," He can't hear us because our actions are speaking too loudly. When we are consciously aware of the Holy Spirit's presence in every moment of our day, God inclines His ear to us, our lives are maximized to glorify our Father in heaven, and we live as He called us to live.

Are there any sins you refuse to give up that are keeping God from inclining His ear to you? What are they, and why are you hanging on to them?

_____

_____

There are so many benefits to prayer, but the last one we will cover today is that prayer gives us wisdom.

Look up James 1:5 and write it here.

_____

_____

If we lack wisdom, what does James suggest we do?

_____

_____

How will God give us wisdom?

_____

_____

The Greek word translated "generously" in James 1:5 is *haplōs,* and it means "bountifully; liberally."[1] God wants to give us wisdom bountifully or liberally. Why should we want wisdom? Let's see what the Bible tells us.

Read Proverbs 3:13. What does this scripture say the one who finds wisdom is?

_____

_____

Read Proverbs 4:5. What does this scripture tell us to get or acquire?

_____

_____

Lastly, read James 3:17. List what wisdom from above is.

_____

_____

_____

Based on what you have just read, what is the benefit of seeking wisdom? What would you like to gain from seeking wisdom?

_____

_____

_____

In Jewish culture, wisdom is very important. Wisdom is not the same as knowledge. You can have knowledge, but if you don't have wisdom, you will not know how to apply the knowledge correctly. Warren Wiersbe describes the distinction this way: "Knowledge is the ability to take things apart, while wisdom is the ability to put them together. Wisdom is the right use of knowledge."[2] If you are going through a trial, it will benefit you to ask God to give you wisdom because He will give it "generously" (Jas. 1:5). When you pray to God in faith, seeking wisdom, He will supply all the wisdom you need.

If you understand nothing else, please know this: Prayer is critical to your walk with Christ. If the enemy can keep you from praying, He can keep you from accomplishing God's will. Brothers and sisters, I don't want you to be far from God. I want your life to be full of everything God has intended for you. I want your prayer life to make the enemy shudder and the impossible a reality. Prayer is our direct access to our Creator, Father, Physician, Restorer, Redeemer, and Friend. Let us pray so that He will incline His ear to us and move on our behalf!

DAY 5

CONNECTING THROUGH PRAYER AND SCRIPTURE

But we will devote ourselves to prayer and to the ministry of the word.

—ACTS 6:4

BEFORE WE BEGIN today, let's pause and pray to the One who is trustworthy and ask Him to reveal truth in our hearts today:

God, as we incline our hearts to You, we now long to bring together the things You have been revealing to us. We long to connect with You through Your Word, and we long to experience the joy of Your presence. Show us how the words You have given us and the words we use to call out to You can bring us into intimacy with You and give us revelation. Amen.

Someone asked an old saint, "Which is more important in my Christian life, praying or studying God's Word?" The saint replied, "Which wing on a bird is more important for his flight, the right one or the left one?" Nothing has built my faith and revealed the Holy Spirit's power to me more than combining prayer with Scripture. When I am going through a tough time, I pray Psalm 121:1–2: "I lift up my eyes to the hills. From where does my help come? My help comes from the LORD, who made heaven and earth." This reminds me that if God made heaven and earth, then He can take care of me and see me through what I am facing.

When we are under attack and the enemy is assaulting us with his lies, we can pray Scripture and destroy those lies with the truth. If we believe God doesn't love us because of unfortunate circumstances, we can pray Romans 8:28: "And we know that God causes all things to work together for good to those who love God, to those who are called according to His purpose" (NASB). When the enemy tells us we are not going to make it through a tough time, we can go to Isaiah 54:17 and declare, "No weapon formed against me will prosper." The only way to overcome the enemy is by the Word of God, and we need to practice using it in our prayer lives.

One of my favorite evangelists was George Müller. He was known for helping orphans but was also a man of prayer and incredible faith. George kept prayer journals, and when he died his journals recorded more than 50,000 prayers that had been answered. When reading through George's journals, I found that his success was dependent on the work the Holy Spirit did when George read God's Word and prayed.

We are studying the unlimited power of the Holy Spirit, and some of the best examples of prayer and power are found in the Book of Acts.

Read Acts 4:31.

What happened when God's people were praying together?

What happened first, the shaking or the praying?

God wants us to remain in a continual posture of prayer. Our motive for praying needs to be a desire to connect with God and have a relationship with Him, not to get Him to fulfill a laundry list of requests. When we study His Word, we discover God's will, and we then build our faith by praying His Word back to Him. As we do this, we will find ourselves accessing the unlimited power of the Holy Spirit.

There was a time when Barbara was going through severe depression, and she occasionally stayed with her parents during this time. When I went to visit her, we would spend time praying together. I remember specifically praying John 15:7 over her. It went something like this: "Father, Your Word says, 'If you abide in me, and my words abide in you, ask whatever you wish, and it will be done for you.' God, we are sinners, and we ask for forgiveness. We know that we abide in

You and Your word abides in us. Father, we are asking for You to heal Barbara of depression." Friends, Barbara was healed of depression! She no longer battles that illness. She lives in the joy of the Lord. Glory to God!

> Read Acts 4:31 again. What happened after the place was shaken?

> Read Acts 2:2. What happened there?

The same group of people was present in both verses. Yesterday's experience does not suffice for today's challenges. The Holy Spirit's activity in our lives is not a one and done. We need to activate His power daily by reading the Word and praying.

Friends, look closely at Acts 4:31: "And when they had prayed, the place where they had gathered together was shaken, and they were all filled with the Holy Spirit and began to speak the word of God with boldness" (NASB). Prayer and Scripture go together. When we connect with God in prayer, we are filled with the Holy Spirit and begin to speak the Word of God. We need to be in God's Word and know God's Word so the Holy Spirit can remind us of it when we need it most and when we need to speak the Word of God to those who do not know Jesus.

We studied earlier this week that all Scripture is inspired by God. We are told in Hebrews 4:12, "For the word of God is living and active and sharper than any two-edged sword, and piercing as far as the division of soul and spirit, of both joints and marrow, and able to judge the thoughts and intentions of the heart" (NASB). Brothers and sisters, if the Word is from God and is living and active and can judge the thoughts and intentions of the heart, then why would we not use it in prayer? Why would we waste our time praying only for our needs when we have been given God's words, which have power and are alive and active? All we need is for God's words to activate the Holy Spirit in our lives and to believe

He can do what He has already promised. If we want God to hear our prayers, we need to listen to what He is saying to us.

Look up Romans 10:17 and write it here.

_____

_____

Our faith is built on prayer. When we listen to what God is telling us, the Holy Spirit brings to memory what He has said. As we pray according to the will of God, we will see Him moving in our lives. Prayer is the difference between the best you can do and the best that God can do. When we remind ourselves what God has promised in His Word while we are in prayer, our faith grows, the place where we gather shakes, and we are *all* filled with the Holy Spirit and speak the Word of God with boldness. *This* is where God is glorified—and that is the purpose of prayer.

REST: TRUST THE HOLY SPIRIT

TAP INTO
GOD'S POWER
week5.unlimitedguide.info

AS WE NEAR the conclusion of our time together, I pray that you would enter that ultimate act of surrender that makes all of this work—trust. Join me in this prayer:

God, the more we learn about You and the more we get to know You, the more we discover just how many reasons we have to trust You. You know we are not good at trusting because it involves relinquishing control. But we also know the character of the One who calls us to trust, so help us to let go and trust even so. Holy Spirit, reveal Yourself to us. Soften our hearts to Your truth and give us wisdom to understand. Amen.

DAY 1
TO KNOW HIM IS TO TRUST HIM

I am the good shepherd. I know my own and my own know
me, just as the Father knows me and I know the Father.

—JOHN 10:14–15

WE HAVE MADE it to week 5. Congratulations! You have done so much hard work! In week 1 we learned about some of the characteristics of the Holy Spirit. In week 2 we started with the letter *R* in the acronym REST. The letter *R* reminds us to receive the Holy Spirit. In week 3 we focused on the *E* (empty and fill our vessels). In week 4 we learned the importance of *S* (study Scripture and pray). This week we are leaning into how to apply the *T*: trust the Holy Spirit.

I realize some of us have a tough time trusting. Whether we had a hard childhood or were in an unhealthy relationship, trust can be difficult if we have been hurt. Often we do not know whom to trust, much less how to trust them. The best way to trust is to really know someone. How can we trust the Holy Spirit? We get to *know* Him.

In my life I have had opportunities to trust people. The people I trust the most are the ones I can be myself around. The more time I spend with them, the more of myself I reveal to them, because the more I get to know them, the more I can trust them.

Another way to trust someone is by considering what they are willing to do to show you how much they value you. How can we trust the Holy Spirit? Let me tell you. He came in the form of man so He could be fully known. He did not hide anything from us. He shared with us all of who He is. Until the moment Jesus died on the cross, the only access mankind had to God was from inside the temple in Jerusalem, behind a veil, after a blood sacrifice had been offered. Then only the high priest was allowed into the holy of holies—*once a year.*

God came in the form of Jesus and died as the final sacrifice for my sin, your sin, our sin—all the sin of the world—and upon Jesus' final breath the veil in the temple tore from top to bottom, permitting us full access to the holy of holies. God has made Himself fully known. Despite our sin, He has made Himself known to us so we will allow Him to know us fully. The funny thing is, He knows us anyway. The Holy Spirit knows it all; He is just a gentleman and will not force Himself on me or you. So, why can we trust the Holy Spirit? *He is trustworthy.*

About seven years ago someone changed my life. I came to know the Holy Spirit on a different level. That is my desire for you—that you will learn more about the Holy Spirit and develop a deep relationship with Him. I pray that you know the Holy Spirit better today than you did five weeks ago.

Let's look and see what the Bible tells us about trusting the Holy Spirit.

Read Ephesians 1:13, 17.

After you believed in Jesus, what happened?

In verse 17, what does the Spirit give you?

In verse 13 the word translated "sealed" is *sphragizō*, meaning "to stamp for security or preservation; by implication, to keep secret, to attest: seal up, stop."[1] This signifies a transaction that is complete and authentic, and no one can break it. It means God has purchased you through the blood of His Son. If you have accepted Jesus as your Savior, you are sealed. You are safe and secure in Him by the blood of Jesus!

Read John 14:16–17.

Who will Jesus give you?

How long will the Helper be with you?

124

What is another name for the Helper used in this passage?

_____

How do you know the Helper?

_____

_____

Friends, do you see that you can know the Holy Spirit? Do you see that you can trust Him? When you accepted Jesus as Lord and Savior of your life, you immediately received the Holy Spirit, and the Spirit of Truth will lead you into the knowledge of Him. This does not mean you receive *all* the knowledge of God at that time. It means you have the power to receive more knowledge of Him as you spend time in His Word and trust Him with every part of your life. British evangelist Leonard Ravenhill said, "To be much for God, we must be much with God."[2] God will never leave you. You can't add Christ to your life without subtracting sin, but once you accept Him, He will never leave you. You are sealed.

Now read John 17:3. This verse talks of knowing God, but not in the sense of having information and facts about Him.

The Greek word used for *know* in this verse is *ginōskō*, which is used to describe intimate knowledge gained through close, personal relationships.[3] It is the same word used to describe the intimate relationship between a husband and wife. When a husband and wife develop a deep, intimate relationship, they grow to know each other well enough to anticipate their spouse's thoughts and actions. As couples grow in *ginōskō*, a transformation takes place in their thoughts, actions, priorities, and values. The Holy Spirit abides in us, and as we develop an intimate relationship with Him, we can anticipate the mind and thoughts of Jesus, and our thoughts, actions, priorities, and values begin to look more like His.

This is the knowledge the Holy Spirit wants to give us in unlimited amounts. Just like Paul prayed in Ephesians 1:18, I pray that the eyes of your heart may be enlightened, so "that you may know the hope to which he has called you." I pray that as you get to know the Holy Spirit more, you will trust Him more so His unlimited power can be released in your life for His glory!

DAY 2
I CAN TRUST HIM TO LEAD ME

For all who are being led by the Spirit of God, these are sons of God.
—ROMANS 8:14, NASB

HELLO, MY FRIEND! Since you are a student of God's Word, let us take a moment to seek God's heart, asking what He would have us take away and apply to our lives for His glory:

God, I have spent too much of my life wandering. The more I come to know You, the more I trust You to lead me—and I surrender myself to Your leadership today that You might guide, nudge, direct, and speak to me. I want to put all my weight down on the sound of Your voice today. Amen.

Today we are talking about the Holy Spirit leading us as we continue to lean into trusting Him. God has blessed me with a wonderful church and an amazing staff to lead. It is an honor to get to love everyone the Lord has brought to Rock Springs Church. I depend on God every day to continue to move in the direction He is taking us. I know the Holy Spirit leads me because I know He loves me. I want to show you some things in the Bible that indicate that the Holy Spirit is leading you too.

Look up Galatians 5:16 and write it here.

_____

_____

What do we do by the Spirit?

_____

What will that prevent us from doing?

The word translated "walk" in Galatians 5:16 is *peripateō*, and it means "to live, deport oneself, follow (as a companion)."[1] We are not alone, and God does not expect us to accomplish His will for us on our own. He sent us the Holy Spirit to help us.

Read Galatians 5:18.

What does this verse say will prevent us from being under the law?

The word *led* in Galatians 5:18 means to be open and receptive to the Holy Spirit's guidance. There are all kinds of behaviors that will keep us from accomplishing God's purpose for our lives, but ultimately fulfilling God's will comes down to allowing the Holy Spirit to lead and guide us in every decision.

I am always asking, "God, lead me." Let me give you an example. One Sunday, my security guy told me he was going to our Macon campus that day. Something did not sit right with me, and I told him I thought he needed to be in Milner instead. That very Sunday, in one of our services, someone started approaching the platform while I was praying. Guess who was able to grab this person who would have caused a huge disturbance during the prayer of salvation? My security guy! Without anyone noticing, he was able to keep this person from disrupting the service and potentially preventing someone from giving their life to Jesus. If the security guy had been in Macon, who knows what disturbance this person could have caused. It is always good to ask God to lead us in every situation.

In the Bible, followers of Jesus are often referred to as sheep. Jesus referred to Himself as the Good Shepherd. (See John 10:11, 14.) We will talk more about shepherds and sheep tomorrow, but I am bringing them up today to discuss David, one of the best-known shepherds in the Bible. Not only was David considered a man after God's own heart, but he was also a good leader and penned one of the most quoted passages in the Bible: Psalm 23.

Ask God to speak a fresh word to you as you read Psalm 23 slowly.

What do you know about sheep?

_____

_____

Why do you think Jesus referred to Himself as the Good Shepherd?

_____

_____

What does this have to do with being led by the Holy Spirit? Sheep are not smart (neither am I), and they need a shepherd (so do I). Sheep need a shepherd to lead them to food, water, and rest. When Jesus says He is our Shepherd, He is saying He will provide for our every need through the Holy Spirit's leading us to Scripture, refreshing our soul, and giving us peace during chaos. Sheep will *not* lie down when they are hungry, and they will *not* drink from a stream that flows quickly. I can relate. I do not sleep well when I am hungry, and if I see a raging river, I am probably not going to stick my head in it to get a drink.

Read Revelation 7:17.

Who is in the center of the throne?

_____

What will He be for those coming out of the tribulation?

_____

Where will He guide these people?

_____

_____

Scripture is consistent. In the Old Testament, David said, "The LORD is my shepherd" who "makes me lie down in green pastures" and "leads me beside still waters" (Ps. 23:1–2). In the New Testament, Jesus said He is the Good Shepherd who "calls his own sheep by name and leads them out" (John 10:3). In the Book of Revelation, Jesus is the Lamb in the center of the throne, the Shepherd who will lead His sheep to the springs of the water of life (Rev. 7:17). When we trust the Shepherd, He leads us to provision and safety because of His love for us.

In Psalm 23:3 the word translated "leads" (*nāhal*) means to lead gently.[2] Sheep hear the shepherd's voice and follow him, but they will not be driven. How do we know the Holy Spirit is leading us? Scripture tells us that as a shepherd loves his sheep, Jesus loved us enough to lay down His life for us. He gently leads us. He is not pushy, and He will not take us where we will not be safe.

Since Jesus, as our Shepherd, laid down His life for us and sent the Holy Spirit to lead us, we should go to Scripture daily, live in obedience to Him, and trust that He will lead us to "green pastures" and "still waters." We will have peace during chaos because we trust the One who is leading us.

With that in view, write John 10:14 here.

_____

_____

Who is the good shepherd?

_____

What or whom does the shepherd know?

_____

To know and be known—this is something I cannot get over. The Lord knows me and wants me to know Him. He knows everything about me—every one of my sins, every undesirable thing about me, every single thing I have done and will do. Why would He want this for me? So I can demonstrate His love to others! I am loved and accepted by the Creator of the world. His hands fashioned me together in my mother's womb. He knows the number of hairs on my head, and He desires to have a relationship with me through the gift of the Holy Spirit. And guess what: He wants the same for you too!

You are loved, accepted, worthy, and adored by God, my friend. Allow Him to lead you in the paths of righteousness for His name's sake! To know and be known by God is the greatest of all trusts, and it is in trusting Him that we can fully love others for His glory—which can only be done with the help of the Holy Spirit.

Great work today!

DAY 3
HOW DO I KNOW HIS VOICE?

So faith comes from hearing, and hearing through the word of Christ.
—ROMANS 10:17

TODAY WE WILL keep our prayer simple:

Lord, give us ears to hear.

We have made it to day 3 in our study of the *T* in REST, trusting the Holy Spirit. We have covered so many topics, and I am so proud of you for sticking with me! Today we are going to focus specifically on trusting the voice of God.

Do you believe God has a voice? Why or why not?

_____

_____

Do you believe God wants to communicate with you? Why or why not?

_____

_____

I have found that many people do not have a hard time believing God sent His Son to die on a cross, but they have trouble believing He loves us enough to send us a message.

In the Bible we see several people who were able to hear God's voice. They put themselves in a position where they were not so distracted that they couldn't hear what He had to say.

What is preventing you from hearing what the Holy Spirit is communicating to you? Doubt? Disobedience? Distractions?

_____

_____

Take a minute and think about an average day. What voices are you listening to? Are you listening to negative self-talk, gossip, social media, or the news? Are you listening to praise music or secular music? How do you think these voices affect you?

_____

_____

What devices do you keep on during the day? Why do you keep those devices on?

_____

_____

Is there any time in your day when it is completely silent? If so, when? If not, why?

_____

_____

_____

I am not saying you should never turn on the radio or TV or listen to friends and family. I am just asking that you stop and think about who or what you are listening to, and if you have made room for the Holy Spirit to speak.

Let us look at how people in the Bible heard the voice of God.

Read 1 Kings 19:4–13.

> Who is the prophet in this story?

_____

> What was Elijah doing?

_____

> When the word of the Lord came to Elijah, what did God ask the prophet to do?

_____

_____

> Go back and read verses 11 and 12 again. How did the Spirit speak to Elijah?

_____

_____

The *Cambridge Dictionary* defines *whisper* as "to speak very quietly, using the breath but not the voice, so that only the person close to you can hear you."[1] Just as Adam was formed with a breath in Genesis, the Holy Spirit spoke to Elijah in a gentle whisper.

With that in view, read Psalm 107:29. The word translated "still" in this verse is the same one translated "whisper" in 1 Kings 19:12. The same voice that formed all of creation speaks to us. Notice that God's voice is not a loud, clamoring noise. We do not hear Him in the hustle and bustle of the day. We hear His voice in the quiet place, when we're alone, waiting in His presence and anticipating Him speaking.

Elijah was not in a good place emotionally in 1 Kings 19. He was depressed and feeling sorry for himself. God cared for his needs, listened to his complaints, asked the hard question, and then spoke to Elijah in a whisper—*a whisper*. Think of the position you must be in to whisper to someone. You must lean in and get close—so close, you are almost touching that person. God spoke to Elijah in a whisper.

What "noise" would you need to turn off to hear the Holy Spirit's voice?

_____

_____

What would you need to cancel from your calendar to be available to hear from the Holy Spirit?

_____

_____

How do you get still? When was the last time you were still?

_____

_____

When you are not in a good place emotionally, what do you typically do or turn to for comfort?

_____

_____

If you turn to anything or anyone other than God, consider getting quiet and waiting with an expectation that you will hear Him whisper to you.

Scripture tells us another way we hear from the Holy Spirit.

Look up John 10:27 and write it here.

_____

_____

The word *voice* in Greek is *phōnē*, and it is defined as "a sound, a tone… speech."[2] It is probably akin to the Greek word *phainō* in the form of disclosure, and it means "to bring forth into the light, cause to shine, shed light, shine, be bright or resplendent, to become evident…come to view, appear."[3]

First, you need to know that a shepherd knows his flock. The shepherd knows each sheep's personality, its likes and dislikes. The shepherd is always counting his sheep because he needs to know if one is lost or injured. When a sheep has been harmed or is sick, the shepherd takes special care of that sheep. When a shepherd cares for the sheep, the sheep learns to trust the shepherd, and it depends on the shepherd more intimately. When the shepherd calls that sheep's name, the sheep immediately responds and trusts its shepherd. The sheep will drink from the shepherd's cup, rub against the shepherd with affection, and follow the shepherd's voice.

Throughout Scripture, God did amazing things through several shepherds. Abel was a shepherd. Abraham was a shepherd. Jacob was a shepherd. Moses was a shepherd. David was a shepherd. Amos was a shepherd. The first announcement about Jesus' arrival was made to shepherds. It should not be surprising to us that Jesus talks about shepherds.

In John 10:27 Jesus is telling His listeners that just as sheep know their shepherd, His followers know His voice. Through the gentle whisper of the Holy Spirit's voice inside us, He will be revealed to us.

How can we be certain we are hearing the voice of the
Holy Spirit?

_____

_____

We know God by His Word. The Holy Spirit brings Scripture to mind—which means it must be hidden in our hearts so He'll have something to pull from—and His voice will never contradict what the Bible says is true.

Like some of the shepherds in Scripture, we also can come to know His voice through our past experiences with Him. God may lead us to do hard things. When He leads us to do hard things, we must make sure we are able to hear what He is trying to communicate to us. He showed up to Moses in a burning bush and to Elijah in a whisper on a mountain.

In their times of trial, these shepherds heard God's voice. They were alone when they heard the Holy Spirit speak. They didn't hear Him while they were scrolling on their phones, watching TV, or busy with activities. He did not speak to them while they were talking to others. The Holy Spirit did not lead them in the direction He wanted them to go while they were trying to impress others. The Holy Spirit spoke to both of these men, who happened to be shepherds, while they were alone in the fields, watching over their flocks.

Shepherds were not highly favored people in their communities. They were not known for having the best clothes or taking the best vacations. Shepherds were not known for having the highest educational background, either. But I believe shepherds were used of God because they knew how to discern the voice of the One calling them, and they trusted Him.

Read John 16:13.

What will the Spirit do?

_____

What will He tell you?

_____

This means the Holy Spirit, the One who dwells inside us, wants to guide us and direct our decision-making. He is always willing to speak into our situations, but we must ask for His guidance and be able to recognize His responses.

The Holy Spirit speaks to us through His Word. It is important that we not only read the Bible but also hide it in our hearts so that we might remember Scripture at just the right time.

Read John 14:26.

What will the Holy Spirit do?

_____

What will the Holy Spirit bring to your remembrance?

_____

Remember, the Holy Spirit can't bring something to our remembrance that we haven't read. If you struggle with memorizing Scripture, we have a page in the back of this study guide with Scripture memorization cards. Cut them out, paste them onto index cards, and carry them around. You will find that if you read the verses over and over—while waiting in lines at school, drive-through lines, or a doctor's office—you will have them memorized in a very short amount of time.

God will also use other godly people to speak to you. David said in 2 Samuel 23:2, "The Spirit of the LORD speaks through me; his words are upon my tongue" (NLT). This means the Holy Spirit can give specific words to people to help guide others in their decision-making.

Read Matthew 10:19–20.

Who gives you the right words?

_____

Who speaks through you?

_____

Surrounding ourselves with godly people is incredibly important because God will often use others to point us in the right direction and to speak truth into our circumstances at just the right time. Attending church regularly, getting involved in a small group, and having a godly mentor are vital to our spiritual growth.

> Do you have someone in your life right now who speaks the truth to you and points you in the right direction? If so, who?

_____

_____

> Do you need to do the hard work of creating space for people of God to get close enough to speak into your life?

_____

God speaks to us in many ways. We need to be able to hear what He is saying. God's greatest desire is to have a relationship with each of us. He sent His Holy Spirit to fellowship with us. *Fellowship* as defined by *Merriam-Webster* is "a friendly relationship" and "a sharing of interest or feeling."[4] The Holy Spirit longs to speak to you because that's what friends do.

One last point before we close today's study: we also know the Holy Spirit's voice because it aligns with His Word and His character.

Read James 1:17.

> What comes down to us from God?

_____

> What did He create?

_____

James 1:17 assures us of God's character. The nineteenth-century preacher Charles Spurgeon once said, "God is too good to be unkind and He is too wise to be mistaken. And when we cannot trace His hand, we must trust His heart."[5] When a confusing or fearful thought comes to your mind, you must ask yourself if the thought aligns with God's Word and character. If it doesn't align, then it must be your own voice or that of the enemy.

Friend, find a quiet place and make yourself available to the Lord. He loves you and wants to speak with you. When we turn off all that the world offers and wait expectantly for God to speak, He often does. His greatest desire is to have a relationship with you. Relationships take time. Make time for the Spirit in your life.

DAY 4
HOW DO I KNOW HIS POWER?

*Now to him who is able to do far more abundantly than
all we ask or think, according to the power at work within
us, to him be glory in the church and in Christ Jesus
throughout all generations, forever and ever. Amen.*

—EPHESIANS 3:20–21

BEFORE WE GET into the material for today, let us take time to thank God for the work He has already done in these last few weeks and ask Him to help us finish strong. May He give us the power and wisdom to understand all the truth He has for us as we continue to learn how to trust the Holy Spirit. Pray with me:

> *God, You have guided me faithfully through the journey so far as my Good Shepherd. I want to use the things You are revealing to bear witness to Your Spirit in the world. As I wait for You in the deep and quiet places, may I come to know You in power to fulfill Your purposes for me in the world. Amen.*

Most of us have turned on an electronic device only to find it not working. Maybe your TV or computer won't turn on, or your earbuds go dead in the middle of a project or workout. It is frustrating when something that is supposed to work doesn't, especially when the problem is that it is not correctly connected to an outlet or has lost power.

So many of us who are followers of Jesus Christ find ourselves in the same position—we think this Christianity thing isn't working when the problem is that we are not connected to the source of our power or we have let our faith go dead.

Read John 15:5.

Apart from God, what can we do?

_____

Paul talks about the power that is available to us so much in his writings in the New Testament. He was passionate that we understand we have spiritual wealth in the Holy Spirit. Through faith in Jesus and the power extended to us we experience God's love and gain the boldness to share His love with all humanity.

Read John 13:1. Then read it again.

Whom did John say Jesus loved?

_____

Do you believe you are part of the group he was referring to? Why or why not?

_____

_____

How long does that love last?

_____

What does love mean to you?

_____

_____

The love spoken of in John 13 is one that is strong, unlimited, and without conditions. It is important that we understand there is not one thing we can do to make God love us any less. He loves each of us despite our wrong decisions and mistakes. He loves each of us despite our past failures and future shortcomings.

It does not matter what we think, what we do, how we treat others, how we treat God—He loves us still.

When we receive the Holy Spirit upon placing our faith in Jesus, we become part of God's work in loving people. As we experience His love through the Holy Spirit, we receive the power to love people and to be witnesses of His love "in Jerusalem, and in all Judea and Samaria, and even to the remotest part of the earth" (Acts 1:8, NASB).

How do we know we have the power of the Holy Spirit? It enables us to do things we cannot do in our own strength.

Read Ephesians 3:20.

What is He able to do?

_____

According to what?

_____

The word translated "power" is *dynamis*, which means "force (literally or figuratively); specially, miraculous power (usually by implication, a miracle itself): ability, abundance, meaning, might, (worker of) miracles, power, strength, violence, mighty (wonderful) work."[1] Now read Ephesians 3:20, quoted here from the New King James Version with the definition of *power* inserted:

> Now to Him who is able to do exceedingly abundantly above all that we ask or think, according to the [*miraculous power, ability, abundance, worker of miracles, strength, mighty work*] that works in us.

Describe the power available to you. Are you accessing that power?

_____

_____

Accessing this power is an act of faith. It is knowing and trusting that God is who He says He is and will do what He says He will do. He has given you access to all that He is through the Holy Spirit. And let's be honest—sometimes we let our batteries die or we forget we have a power source to plug into. How do we know we have access to the Holy Spirit's power? Scripture tells us we do! Let us look at a few more verses so we have no doubt.

Read 2 Peter 1:3–4.

His power has granted to us what?

Having escaped what?

Do you see here that we are called to life and godliness and have escaped the corruption that is in the world by lust? Friend, that is power! That is unlimited power! How do you know you have power in the Holy Spirit? You can resist things of this world. And *if* you fall into sin, the Holy Spirit is there to convict you so you can ask for forgiveness and be right back in fellowship with God in order to be a partaker of the divine nature (2 Pet. 1:3). That is the unlimited power of the Holy Spirit working in you and me. Amen! I could jump out of my seat just thinking about it.

You may be asking, "How do I know when to use this power?" I believe we need this power every second of every day. There is a spiritual battle going on around us, whether we choose to acknowledge it or not. I wake up every day to three enemies: the world, the flesh, and the devil. We have a very real enemy who wants to destroy our lives and make us hopeless.

Read 1 Peter 5:8.

Who is the enemy?

What does the enemy do?

_____

Our enemy is very real, and if we want to be prepared for battle, we must be familiar with him as well as our greatest weapon and our strongest defense—the Holy Spirit. But first, let's learn to understand our enemy.

Read John 10:10, focusing on the first half of the verse.

Who comes?

_____

What does he come to do?

_____

Our enemy has no new tactics. His strategy is deception: distorting the truth and telling lies. He attacks our minds and promotes sin, immoral lifestyles, and unrealistic standards to steal our peace. He also uses stress and exhaustion to distract and overwhelm us so we don't even realize our focus has shifted from God's purpose for our lives to our daily plans.

What tactic is the enemy currently using to shift your focus away from your divine purpose?

_____

_____

What is our power against these kinds of tactics? It is the power of the Holy Spirit!

Let's read Romans 8:13.

If you are living by the flesh, the enemy is working hard. According to this scripture, how are we to put our fleshly desires away?

_____

What do we gain by living this way?

_____

When we rely on the unlimited power of the Holy Spirit, He will help us recognize the enemy's lies, and His presence will make our hearts sensitive to His promptings to flee from temptation or to say no when our lives get too busy. The Holy Spirit will bring truth to every situation, defend you in every battle, and lead you to victory because He has a great plan and purpose for your life!

Romans 8:37 says, "No, in all these things we are more than conquerors through him who loved us." We do not have to accept defeat in our lives. We need to plug into the power source that gives us life, become partakers of God's divine nature, and use the power of the Holy Spirit to love others as we are loved and reach the world for Jesus!

DAY 5
FOLLOW CLOSELY

*And calling the crowd to him with his disciples, he said to
them, "If anyone would come after me, let him deny himself and take up his cross and follow me."*

—MARK 8:34

ET IN A quiet place and turn your heart to Jesus. Ask Him to use this time to direct your steps to walk intimately with Him according to His Word and will. We praise You, Jesus, for all that You are going to do in our time together today! Pray this prayer with me:

*God, as You have drawn me to You on the road thus far, it is my
desire now to draw even closer. I want to know the grace of proximity,
to know Your nearness. Grant me the assurance of Your presence that
I may attend to the things You speak to me in the quiet. Amen.*

When a couple first starts dating, they usually spend a lot of time together to get to know each other better. Both parties usually begin the relationship by putting their best foot forward and trying to avoid doing anything that would upset the other person. They like being close. When the couple is close, they learn each other's patterns, likes, and dislikes. Over time the couple begins to use the same language and phrases. Some couples do not even have to speak to each other; they can read each other's body language. There is a trust that is built over time, and that trust will see the couple through the most difficult days.

It is the same in your relationship with the Holy Spirit. We have spent time over the last five weeks talking about things that quench the Holy Spirit or keep Him from having unlimited power in our lives. Just as trust is broken when we lie to our spouse or act in a way that does not build him or her up, so can our actions hinder our relationship with the Holy Spirit. We cannot sin against God and follow the Holy Spirit closely. If you do not feel you are following the Holy Spirit closely, I can promise you one thing—the Holy Spirit is not the one who has moved.

Let's look to the Bible to see what it teaches about following the Holy Spirit closely. There are a few men in Scripture who were commended for their walks with God.

Read Genesis 5:22–24.

Who walked with God?

_____

How did Enoch die?

_____

How many times did these verses say "walked with God"?

_____

Enoch walked with God, not with the world, and God rewarded him by taking him. Before and after verses 22–24 you will see the phrase "and he died" written about everyone—except Enoch. I cannot promise you that you will not die, but my point here is that God notices those who follow (walk with) Him closely.

Read Genesis 6:9.

Who walked with God here?

_____

I strongly encourage you to read the account of Noah in Genesis 6–9. But for now, read Genesis 6:22 and 7:5, 9, 16.

How did Noah respond to God's command?

_____

Read Genesis 9:1.

What did God do?

_____

Who was blessed?

_____

Notice that Noah and his sons were blessed and only Noah was commended for doing "all that the LORD had commanded him" (7:5).

To follow closely is to do God's will. When we obey God's will, we give the Holy Spirit unlimited access to work in our lives. By following Him closely and trusting the Holy Spirit, our lives are full in God. Our lives won't be easy or perfect, but they will be what God has planned for us.

Let's go to the New Testament and see what Jesus has to say.

Read Mark 8:34.

What does Jesus say we should do if we want to follow Him?

_____

I want to make sure that we stay in context with the Scripture here. At this point in Jesus' ministry there were many people following Him because of the miracles He was performing. Jesus was alone with His disciples at this point in Mark 8, and He took the opportunity to teach them something. He wanted those closest to Him to know that following Him came with a price.

Closely following the Holy Spirit often comes at a price, and Jesus spells it out for us here in Mark 8:34. What is the cost? We must surrender ourselves completely to Him, identify with Him in suffering and death, and be obedient to go wherever He leads, whenever He calls. I can tell you from experience that God is not always on my schedule and His timing is not often convenient for me. Surrendering to His will and following Him closely means making the most of our opportunities here on earth to glorify Him. The reward for following Jesus is that we look more like Him!

Read John 8:12.

What is the promise here for those who follow Jesus?

_____

Jesus is asking us to believe in and trust Him. Do you trust Him? Why or why not?

_____

_____

Our following Jesus depends on how deeply we trust Him. As this scripture teaches us, if we believe in Him and trust Him, we will have light and life. Our ability to follow the Holy Spirit closely lies in our willingness to confess sin, repent, and seek restoration.

We follow the Holy Spirit closely by developing an intentional relationship with Him.

What prevents you from walking closely with the Holy Spirit?

_____

_____

Without completely surrendering to the Holy Spirit daily and relying on a fresh infilling of His power, you leave yourself vulnerable to the enemy's attacks. On your own you are no match for the enemy's deceitful tactics. But with the Holy Spirit you have power to overcome the enemy.

Even those closest to Jesus struggled to follow Him. When a person's spirit is right with the Lord, there is closeness, intimacy, and joy that cannot be felt through any earthly relationship. Follow the Holy Spirit closely. In Him there is light and life!

BENEFITS OF THE HOLY SPIRIT

TAP INTO GOD'S POWER
week6.unlimitedguide.info

AS WE DRAW closer to the end of our time together, I want you to focus on the tangible ways God will enhance your life as you walk in the fullness of His Spirit. As we've been doing throughout our study, let us enter this last leg of the journey from a prayerful posture. Pray with me:

God, as we have come to trust Your heart and intentions for us, we want to be even clearer in our vision of what You have for us. Show us the good things You have in store for us as Your children that we might trust Your voice as Your words light our path. From the exodus forward You have always been on the move as the God of freedom. Teach us to trust You, liberating God, as You set us free to reveal Your goodness to the world around us. Amen.

DAY 1
LIVING FREE

*Now the Lord is the Spirit, and where the Spirit
of the Lord is, there is freedom.*

—2 Corinthians 3:17

On January 6, 1941, President Franklin D. Roosevelt shared a vision with Congress of four basic freedoms all people should enjoy: freedom of speech, freedom of worship, freedom from want, and freedom from fear. For the most part, these freedoms have been achieved here in the United States. However, we all need another kind of freedom—freedom from ourselves and our sinful nature. Because God sent His Son, Jesus, to die for our sins and He was resurrected on the third day, the Holy Spirit has come, and we now have access to that freedom! We have unlimited power through the Holy Spirit to no longer be slaves to our flesh.

Read Romans 8:1–2.

If we believe in Jesus, what are we free from?

_____

What gives us that freedom?

_____

This is such great news! While I believe most Christians experience salvation and truly believe their sins are forgiven, many struggle to let themselves live in freedom.

What are some things that keep us from living free?

_____

_____

Describe how the "chains" of fear or human limitations impact you.

_____

_____

_____

How about what others say about you or labels that have been placed on you? Describe the impact words have had on you.

_____

_____

_____

Are there generational sins that have not been addressed in your family line that keep you from living the life Jesus has promised you through the Holy Spirit? What are they? What would it take for you to break free from those?

_____

_____

_____

If we listen to any voice other than God's, we are living a limited life.

What has the Holy Spirit been saying to you about His will for your life through this study guide?

_____

_____

My salvation experience was real, and I meant every word of the prayer I prayed—but I didn't wake up the next morning free of all my bad habits and sinful behaviors. On the night I was saved, I was forgiven. But I am still convicted today for the sins I commit daily. I am not the only one, and neither are you. Let's look back in history to the Jewish people. It took God one day to get the Israelites out of Egypt, but it took Him forty years to get Egypt out of them.

The Israelites had been slaves for hundreds of years. They had lived under the strong forces of Egypt and worked as hard laborers. Pharaoh had ordered their firstborn to be killed. They had been abused, talked down to, and told their daily labor was not sufficient. It was clear Israel needed to be rescued. God led them out and promised to lead them to a land filled with milk and honey.

It did not take Israel long after their rescue to start complaining as they traveled in the wilderness. Yet God took care of their needs while they were there, and He told them to build a sanctuary so He could dwell among them. This sanctuary came with very specific instructions. While God was telling Moses how the sanctuary should be constructed, He instructed Moses to take a census.

Read Exodus 30:7–12 and notice when God called for the census during the instructions. God asked Israel to build an altar of incense where atonement would be made for sins once a year; _then_ He asked Moses to take a census. The Hebrew word translated "census" in Exodus 30:12 is _rō'š_, and it means "from an unused root apparently meaning to shake; the head (as most easily shaken)."[1] In essence, God asked Moses to go to each person in the community and lift his or her head. When you gently lift the chin of someone who is shaking or cast down, that person will look you in the face. Looking someone in the eye tells them they matter. God wanted His people to know that they mattered and had worth. They had been worn down, having been enslaved their entire lives. God delivered them from Egypt and provided a way for them to be cleansed from their sins; then He reminded them of their worth to Him.

When you read farther, to Exodus 30:17–21, you see that God told Moses to make a basin of bronze for washing. This basin was made from mirrors. It was like God was telling them, "Don't look to yourself for your worth; look to Me. I provide atonement. Look to Me, and I will cleanse you because you matter to Me."

God provides atonement. He provides for the cleansing of sin. But in the middle of atonement and cleansing, He wants you and me to know we matter. He wants us to lift our heads and look at Him. When we feel like we are not enough, when we have been in bondage to some addiction, when we have so much shame from bad decisions, the Holy Spirit comes to us and gently lifts our heads (takes a census) and says, "You matter, you are loved, and you have worth."

I had a lot of Egypt still in me after I asked Jesus to come into my life. I needed freedom. I needed the Holy Spirit to gently let me know sin had no residence in my life and that through His power I had strength to overcome and make it to my own promised land.

Do you still have a lot of Egypt in you? What are you still enslaved to?

_____

_____

_____

Have you been told you are not enough? By whom? What does God want you to believe?

_____

_____

_____

What do you need to be rescued from?

_____

_____

When the Holy Spirit is telling you to look up, what makes it hard to lift your head?

_____

_____

Freedom doesn't happen overnight; it is a continual process. That is why Jesus sent us a Helper. We will all learn, grow, and develop in our walk with Christ in unique ways throughout every stage of our lives. The key is surrendering to the power of the Holy Spirit. In surrendering to the Holy Spirit, we allow God to be the lifter of our heads and tell us that we count. We matter. We no longer need to curate an image; we are His reflection, and the Holy Spirit inside us lovingly encourages us to freely give our minds and hearts to Jesus because we are loved by Him!

Look up Psalm 51:10–11 and write it here.

_____

_____

What does this scripture encourage us to ask for?

_____

When the Holy Spirit comes into your life, He doesn't bring supplies to dust off your dirty heart; instead, He creates a new heart within you. He wants to bring freedom and renewal to every person. We are all works in progress, and we need a fresh infilling of the Holy Spirit daily to bring lasting freedom in Jesus.

When you ask the Holy Spirit to fill you with His power and presence each day, He begins to transform your mind by giving you entirely new ways to think about things. He's not interested in doing a little spring cleaning by tidying up your thoughts and getting rid of things that are no longer of use. The Holy Spirit is all about making new creations. He makes all things new!

As you continue walking in the Spirit and allow Him to lead you moment by moment, undeniable change will occur in your heart over time. You won't wake up one morning to find the fruit of the Spirit has miraculously ripened overnight. Instead, you will gradually begin to experience freedom that affects your countenance, conduct, and character.

God wants you to live in freedom, not to be bound by fear and limitations. He wants you to remember He has given you the Holy Spirit to lead you in the path of freedom. You are a child of the Most High, not a slave who is tormented by enemy attacks. You are chosen, forgiven, loved, favored, and equipped by God. He has great plans for your life. Access His power through a close, intentional relationship with the Holy Spirit so you can overcome fear and be free indeed!

DAY 2
FRESH ANOINTING

I shall be anointed with fresh oil.
—PSALM 92:10, KJV

As we continue in our last week together, let's again begin this day in prayer:

Jesus, I love You, and I pray that You will help me see You through today's study. Help me to understand Your Word and be empowered to proclaim the gospel. Amen.

I understand that some of us see the word *anointing* and are just not sure about it. Maybe it is because we were not raised hearing or experiencing it. Maybe you are uncomfortable because you came from a background that talked about the anointing, but you had a bad experience. If you are one of those people who doesn't really like the word, or if it makes you uncomfortable, please stick with me and let me show you what the Bible says.

Let us start with Jesus. Read Matthew 1:16.

What did Matthew call Jesus in this verse?

_____

"Christ" or "Messiah" in Greek is *christos*, meaning "anointed" or "anointed one."[1] It is a title. When we say "Jesus Christ," we are not calling Him by a first and last name. We are saying, "Jesus the Anointed One"—and the Anointed One wants to give an anointing to you.

So, you may ask, "Benny, what is an anointing?" Anointing is when the Holy Spirit gives you supernatural wisdom, insight, ability, stamina, or protection to do what He has chosen you to do. There is a calling on every person's life. You were created on purpose for a purpose. We will talk more in depth about our purpose tomorrow, but know that the Holy Spirit is the empowerment God uses to accomplish His work through you. You can never fulfill the call of God in your own power. You need the power of the Holy Spirit and a fresh anointing on your life to fulfill His purpose.

Read 2 Corinthians 1:21–22.

Who establishes you in Christ?

_____

What does God do after we are established in Christ?

_____

_____

What happens after we are anointed?

_____

_____

Friends, this is such good news for us! In the Old Testament only the prophets, priests, and kings were anointed, and it was to equip them for service. Since Jesus came and sent us His Spirit, all of us who follow Him have been anointed by the Holy Spirit. We are *all* able to serve God and live godly lives as we yield to His will. Glory to God!

Read Psalm 23:5.

After God prepared the table before us in the presence of our enemies, what did He do?

_____

_____

Sometimes shepherds would find flat places in the hills to take the sheep to rest. These places were called "tables." This could be what the author is referring to in Psalm 23. After the sheep eat, they sleep. The shepherd had to protect the flock from predators in the places where they took the sheep to find grass or other food. So, after the sheep ate and were lying down, the shepherd would check to make sure they were all accounted for. Then he would check their condition and tend to any injuries or illness.

Another thing the shepherd would do is apply oil to each sheep's head to keep flies and insects away. Why is that important? Sheep are susceptible to flies traveling up their noses and laying eggs that turn into worms that burrow up into the animal's brain. When this happens, the sheep will bang their heads to the point of death to get rid of the irritation. The oil keeps the flies and insects from going in. Sheep also butt heads, and while the shepherds can't always prevent it from happening, the oil keeps the sheep from doing themselves or others much harm.

> After learning all of this, why do you think we need a fresh anointing?

_____

_____

We are all like sheep. We have irritations in our lives that make us feel like butting our heads until we do damage. The Holy Spirit in us helps direct our minds to a healthy place that keeps the irritations at a minimum. And as far as butting heads with other sheep, that happens all too often. But as it is with natural sheep, a fresh anointing can prevent us from getting harmed too badly. I need a fresh anointing several times a day on some days. What about you?

DAY 3
PURPOSE

*The LORD will fulfill his purpose for me; your stead-
fast love, O LORD, endures forever.*
—PSALM 138:8

TAKE A MOMENT and quietly reflect on God's grace and goodness. Praise Him for being our Creator, Sustainer, and the Giver of all good things! Pray this prayer with me:

God, there are so many ways You have shown Your goodness to me, so many ways You continue to demonstrate Your faithfulness to me. Grant me clarity today to see who You have called me to be and what You have called me to do by the power of Your Holy Spirit. Amen.

God is faithful to teach us about the true power of the Holy Spirit to give us divine direction. His plan is better than any path we could make for ourselves. No matter how long you've been a Christian or how many scriptures you've memorized, you cannot fulfill your purpose without the Holy Spirit guiding you every day.

The Holy Spirit calls us to a life of humility and selflessness because our true purpose will always be tied to other people. Let's look at Romans 8:28 (NASB). We like the line "God causes all things to work together for good"—but read a bit farther. He works things together for those who are called to what? His purpose! What is His purpose? In Greek the word is *prothesis*, meaning "a setting forth...specifically, the show-bread (in the Temple) as exposed before God."[1]

Are you thinking, "Benny, I have no idea what you are talking about"? Let me explain: "And we know that for those who love God all things work together for good, for those who are called according to his purpose" (Rom. 8:28). Friend, the showbread was set on a table in the tabernacle, and the requirements for the showbread were that there was to be no leaven in the bread, there were to be twelve loaves (one to represent each tribe of Israel), and only the priests could replace it each week. The showbread was a reminder of God's provision for His people. (See Exodus 25:23–30.)

Move into the New Testament, and Jesus tells us He is the Bread of Life. (See week 4, day 1.) Listen close: We are called according to His promise to provide the Bread of Life for our sustenance. That is our purpose—to know Jesus and make Him known. He is our Provider and Sustainer! All things work together for good for those who are His! That is some good news!

So, God has given us all a clear purpose for our lives—to know God and make Him known—and He has given the Holy Spirit to amplify our gifts to advance His purpose.

To know God is most important. If we do not know God, then the Holy Spirit does not dwell in us, and we cannot appropriately lead others to Jesus. I want to be clear: God does not need us; He chooses us to be a part of His work.

Read Matthew 4:19.

What did Jesus ask the disciples to do?

_____

If the disciples followed, what did Jesus say He would make them?

_____

First the disciples had to choose to follow Jesus, and *then* He would send them to disciple others. Jesus was saying, "Know Me, and then you can make Me known." There is always order in the way God does things!

Do you remember when you first asked Jesus into your heart? Use the space provided to recall that experience.

_____

_____

I remember asking Jesus into my heart and telling myself I was going to keep my experience to myself. That lasted until I met up with my friends. When we know Jesus, we want to tell others about Him. To know Him is to make Him known. To tell others about Him is discipleship.

There are two key elements of discipleship.

Read Matthew 28:18–20.

What are we commanded to do?

_____

_____

What are we to teach?

_____

Who is with us?

_____

How is Jesus with us?

_____

How long is He with us?

_____

Read 2 Timothy 1:9.

What did God call us to?

_____

Why did He call us to this life?

_____

What power do we need to live this life?

We are to make disciples and live worthy of our calling, which means to live in such a way that other people see that Jesus is our Provider and Sustainer. Our ultimate purpose is to live a holy life that glorifies God.

God has a specific purpose for every person. You can be sure that when God appoints you, He anoints you. Where God guides, He provides. The Holy Spirit gives supernatural wisdom, ability, stamina, and protection for us to do His will. We can't accomplish anything of significance without the power of the Holy Spirit. The Bible tells us there are three things we should not be ignorant concerning: the second coming of Christ (1 Thess. 4:13–18), the devices of the devil (2 Cor. 2:11, KJV), and our spiritual gifts (1 Cor. 12:1). Life is so important, and it's vital that we know how the Holy Spirit has specifically gifted us. Spiritual gifts are unique to each believer. Your spiritual gifts have an eternal purpose!

> Why are we given spiritual gifts? Read 1 Peter 4:10–11 and list the two reasons given.

To serve others and glorify God—that is why we are given spiritual gifts. We will find it difficult to discover our purpose if we are focusing on the person in the mirror.

> How does it make you feel to know the Holy Spirit has given you gifts for a unique purpose?

If you do not know your spiritual gifts, see the appendix, where you will find links to spiritual gifts tests. Visit one of the websites and take the test to see how God has created you to serve others. As you begin to serve in the manner for which God created you, you will find more satisfaction in your walk with the Holy Spirit, and you will see His unlimited power manifest in your life.

Never forget that you were created on purpose for an unlimited purpose! When you seek closeness with the Holy Spirit and completely surrender to His plans, He will equip you for the most exciting journey you could ever take. He has the best plans for you—but don't forget that when He calls you and blesses you, He has more than you in mind. You are a vital part of the body of Christ, and the church needs each person's gift to be fully operational!

Friend, step into your purpose because you are well equipped and mission ready. You have the unlimited power of the Holy Spirit!

DAY 4
PEACE

Now may the Lord of peace Himself continually grant you
peace in every circumstance. The Lord be with you all!
—2 THESSALONIANS 3:16, NASB

BEFORE WE TALK about the peace that only comes from God, let's take a moment to pray:

Father, I want to know You more! Make Yourself known to me today as I study Your Word!

I love taking groups to Israel. I love walking in the places where the Bible comes to life. I love teaching God's Word where the Scriptures come to life. Many times when I walk the streets of Jerusalem, people greet me by saying "Shalom." To the Jewish people, this word is precious. It is the Hebrew word for *peace*, but to the Jewish people it also means wholeness, completeness, health, security, and even prosperity.

The world today does not show us much peace. But Jesus tells us in John 16:33, "These things I have spoken to you, that in Me you may have peace" (NKJV). We must not look at our circumstances to find peace; we must look to the One who is the Giver of peace.

Read John 14:27.

What did Jesus leave us?

_____

What did Jesus give us?

_____

The world gives us trouble (*tarassō*: "to stir or agitate"[1]) and fear. Jesus gives us peace. The word Jesus uses in John 14:27 is *eirēnē*, meaning "quietness," "harmony," "security, safety."[2] Look at how different what the world gives is from what Jesus offers. Which do you prefer? Another benefit of having the power of the Holy Spirit is that He gives us peace. The world has us tossing back and forth, feeling unsettled, unsafe, and insecure. When we put our trust in Jesus, it does not matter what the world throws at us—He has overcome it all, and we can feel protected.

Read Colossians 3:15.

Where does peace come from?

The word *rule* used in Colossians 3:15 means to act as an umpire.[3] The Holy Spirit lets us know when something is not right in our lives. Through his letter to the Colossians, Paul is telling us we need to let the peace of Christ act as an umpire, and if our "gut," or inner self, is not at peace, we need to address the sin "and be thankful."

Sometimes we lack peace because we are not right with God. When we are disobedient to what He has asked us to do, the Holy Spirit convicts us to let us know we need to confess the sin and ask for forgiveness. The peace Jesus gives springs out of our ability to be in right standing with our Father in heaven, and that is a reason to be grateful.

Read Ephesians 4:1–6.

What should we make every effort to do?

By being united with the Spirit, what are we binding ourselves to?

Because of God's great love for us, He has greatly blessed us. Because He has blessed us so extravagantly through the gift of His Son and the Holy Spirit, our response as the body of Christ should be to live in obedience to Him and show the world that His people can live together in unity through the bond of peace. When we can keep our inside at peace with the help of the Holy Spirit, it is easier to maintain peace with the outside world.

Brothers and sisters, we need to allow the Holy Spirit full access to our lives to show a lost and hurting world what unity in the Spirit looks like and reach them for Jesus!

DAY 5
HE CALLS ME FRIEND

But there is a friend who sticks closer than a brother.
—**PROVERBS 18:24**

CONGRATULATIONS! YOU MADE it to the last day of our study. I wish I could sit with you and hear what God has shown you in the last six weeks. His love for you is immeasurable, and you are precious to Him. One last time together, let us praise God for the great things He has done. Let's ask Him to meet us where we are and to bless us with His unlimited power and presence:

God, thank You that You do not speak to us as servants. You do not shout to us from afar. You whisper to us close. In intimacy with You, we find joy. Thank You for calling us friends. May we know the fullness of life that can be found only in friendship with You. Amen.

I have been married to Barbara for forty years now as of the release of this book. I can tell you I love her more today than I did the day we got married. That does not mean we have had a perfect marriage, because we have not. It means the longer I live with her and share life experiences, the more I trust her. The more I trust her, the more I love her. Friends, our relationship with the Holy Spirit works similarly.

As we conclude our time together in this study today, I want you to know that God has been seeking an intimate relationship with you since before creation. You are so loved that He has literally moved heaven and earth to make a way to know you. He has protected a family line since Adam so He could give us Jesus in the form of man. He cannot look upon sin, so He gave us a foreshadowing of a perfect blood sacrifice in a Temple (where He dwelled among His people) so we would recognize the sacrifice that was paid for each one of us. After Jesus lived a perfect life and died for all our sins so we could have free access to the throne of God, He sent the Holy Spirit to live (tabernacle) in each of us who believes in Jesus Christ. He did all this because He so loves you and me!

With that in mind, read John 15:12–17.

What is the greatest display of love?

_____

_____

What does Jesus call us?

_____

What has Jesus made known to us?

_____

Write John 15:16.

_____

_____

Have you ever been the last one chosen on the playground? Have you ever not been invited to an event that everyone else you knew was attending? Have you ever felt like you were less than in any capacity? Friends, Jesus tells us that we are *chosen*! That's right; He chose you! You are on His team. You are invited to His party! The Lamb will be having a wedding supper (Rev. 19:9), and you made the list! You are His bride, and He is coming back to take you to be with Him for all eternity! Let us give Him praise and glory!

God calls you His friend. Let that sit with you just a minute. God loves you despite you! God loves me despite me! He has a unique plan and purpose for each of us, and He sent His Holy Spirit to live inside you to renovate and remodel His dwelling place so others will want to know the peace that comes only from Him. If you allow the Holy Spirit complete access, He will redeem and restore you to active duty in sharing the gospel and ministering to others.

Look up Psalm 51:12–13 and write it here.

_____

_____

Take a minute and pray that passage. Make an honest confession to God about what you would like restored. Ask Him for the courage to be obedient to *whatever* the Holy Spirit is asking you to do. Confess that you cannot do anything apart from Him. Ask Him to restore to you the joy of His salvation. James 2 tells us "the Scripture was fulfilled which says, 'And Abraham believed God, and it was reckoned to him as righteousness,' and he was called the friend of God" (v. 23, NASB). Our belief in Jesus and our confession of sins (obedience to His law) leads us into right standing with God (righteousness), and we too are friends of God. He is faithful to do it through the unlimited power of the Holy Spirit!

In conclusion, I pray that after spending six weeks studying the Holy Spirit, you understand His role in your life and have a desire to give Him complete access to your life. I pray that you also understand that since before the creation in Genesis 1, God's desire has been to have an intimate relationship with each of us. He knew we would sin. He knew we would reject Him. He knew we would never be perfect after the fall of man in the Garden of Eden.

After God led Israel out of Egypt, He gave them instructions for building a dwelling place so He could be with His people. The temple was destroyed many times, yet God's desire to dwell with His people remained. He still had a plan—that plan was His only begotten Son. This Son would enter this world in a lowly manger and live a sinless life, die for our sins, and be resurrected so that we could have eternal life through Him.

Before Jesus ascended to heaven, He promised to send the Holy Spirit. On the day of Pentecost, He sent the Holy Spirit, and now the Holy Spirit dwells in each of us who claim Jesus as our Lord and Savior. Now the Holy Spirit lives in us to direct us, comfort us, advocate for us, and help us in our times of deepest need.

The Holy Spirit lives in us and supplies us with unlimited courage, unlimited power, unlimited knowledge, and unlimited resources.

The Holy Spirit was given so God's glory would be revealed to a lost and hurting world. The Holy Spirit chooses you and me to be His home, and He is available to each of us to make us more effective witnesses for Christ. The unlimited power of the Holy Spirit is available to each of us today! All we need to do is give Him unlimited access to our lives and be obedient to what He asks us to do. When we do, we will have access to the wisdom, knowledge, and power of God, and we will live the life Jesus promised in John 10:10—the abundant life!

You are more than a conqueror; you are a child of the living God! Live in the unlimited power of the Holy Spirit!

APPENDIX

THE ACTS PRAYER PLAN

In week 4 we learned about prayer. If you do not know how to pray, consider using what I call the ACTS plan:

1. **A**doration: Begin by praising the Lord.

2. **C**onfess: Ask God to forgive you for the sin in your life. God will show you what you need to correct.

3. **T**hanksgiving: Then thank God for the blessings and goodness in your life.

4. **S**upplication: Finally, bring your needs to the Lord.

SPIRITUAL GIFTS TEST

If you are interested in discovering your spiritual gifts, visit www.giftstest.com or www.spiritualgiftstest.com to take an assessment. Once you identify your spiritual gifts, I encourage you to continue learning more about your gifts and to seek opportunities to use them. If you are not already involved in a local church, I encourage you to get involved and seek ways to serve within the congregation using your spiritual gifts!

SALVATION

For more information on salvation, please visit www.MadeNew.info.

SCRIPTURE MEMORIZATION CARDS

Week 1

"You will receive power when the Holy Spirit has come upon you; and you shall be My witnesses both in Jerusalem, and in all Judea and Samaria, and even to the remotest part of the earth"
(Acts 1:8, NASB).

Week 2

"Behold, I stand at the door and knock; if anyone hears My voice and opens the door, I will come in to him and will dine with him, and he with Me"
(Revelation 3:20, NASB).

Week 3

"It is the Spirit who gives life; the flesh profits nothing; the words that I have spoken to you are spirit and are life"
(John 6:63, NASB).

Week 4

"But we will devote ourselves to prayer and to the ministry of the word"
(Acts 6:4).

Week 5

"Blessed is the man who trusts in the LORD and whose trust is the LORD"
(Jeremiah 17:7).

Week 6

"'As for Me, this is My covenant with them,' says the LORD: 'My Spirit which is upon you, and My words which I have put in your mouth shall not depart from your mouth, nor from the mouth of your offspring, nor from the mouth of your offspring's offspring,' says the LORD, 'from now and forever'"
(Isaiah 59:21).

Week 2

"Behold, I stand at the door and
knock; if anyone hears My voice
and opens the door, I will come in
to him and will dine with him,
and he with Me"
(Revelation 3:20, NASB).

Week 1

"You will receive power when the
Holy Spirit has come upon you;
and you shall be My witnesses both
in Jerusalem, and in all Judea and
Samaria, and even to the remotest
part of the earth"
(Acts 1:8, NASB).

Week 4

"But we will devote ourselves
to prayer and to the ministry
of the word"
(Acts 6:4).

Week 3

"It is the Spirit who gives life;
the flesh profits nothing; the words
that I have spoken to you are spirit
and are life"
(John 6:63, NASB).

Week 6

"'As for Me, this is My covenant
with them,' says the LORD: 'My
Spirit which is upon you, and My
words which I have put in your
mouth shall not depart from your
mouth, nor from the mouth of your
offspring, nor from the mouth of
your offspring's offspring,' says the
LORD, 'from now and forever'"
(Isaiah 59:21).

Week 5

"Blessed is the man who trusts
in the LORD and whose trust
is the LORD"
(Jeremiah 17:7).

NOTES

INTRODUCTION

1. Warren W. Wiersbe, *The Wiersbe Bible Commentary: New Testament* (Colorado Springs, CO: David C. Cook, 2007), 1044.

WEEK 1, DAY 1

1. Blue Letter Bible, s.v. "*rûah*," accessed June 17, 2024, https://www.blueletterbible.org/lexicon/h7307/esv/wlc/0-1/.
2. Blue Letter Bible, s.v. "*pneuma*," accessed June 17, 2024, https://www.blueletterbible.org/lexicon/g4151/esv/mgnt/0-1/.
3. Blue Letter Bible, s.v. "*pneō*," accessed June 17, 2024, https://www.blueletterbible.org/lexicon/g4154/esv/mgnt/0-1/.
4. Blue Letter Bible, s.v. "*pnoē*," accessed June 17, 2024, http://www.blueletterbible.org/lexicon/g4157/esv/mgnt/0-1/.
5. Blue Letter Bible, s.v. "*zōē*," accessed June 17, 2024, http://www.blueletterbible.org/lexicon/g2222/esv/mgnt/0-1/.
6. "Oswald Chambers," AZ Quotes, accessed June 17, 2024, https://www.azquotes.com/quote/827729.

WEEK 1, DAY 2

1. Blue Letter Bible, s.v. "*paraklētos*," accessed June 17, 2024, https://www.blueletterbible.org/lexicon/g3875/esv/tr/0-1/.

WEEK 1, DAY 3

1. Blue Letter Bible, s.v. "*theopneustos*," accessed June 17, 2024, https://www.blueletterbible.org/lexicon/g2315/esv/tr/0-1/.
2. Blue Letter Bible, s.v. "*chrisma*," accessed June 17, 2024, https://www.blueletterbible.org/lexicon/g5545/esv/tr/0-1/.
3. Wiersbe, *The Wiersbe Bible Commentary*, 981.
4. Blue Letter Bible, s.v. "*pas*," accessed June 17, 2024, https://www.blueletterbible.org/lexicon/g3956/esv/tr/0-1/.

WEEK 1, DAY 4

1. "Dwight L. Moody," AZ Quotes, accessed June 17, 2024, https://www.azquotes.com/quote/1395355.
2. Blue Letter Bible, s.v. "*dipsaō*," accessed June 17, 2024, https://www.blueletterbible.org/lexicon/g1372/esv/tr/0-1/.
3. Blue Letter Bible, s.v. "*pinō*," accessed June 17, 2024, https://www.blueletterbible.org/lexicon/g4095/esv/tr/0-1/.

WEEK 2, DAY 1

1. Blue Letter Bible, s.v. "*lambanō*," accessed June 17, 2024, https://www.blueletterbible.org/lexicon/g2983/esv/tr/0-1/.
2. Blue Letter Bible, s.v. "*lambanō*."
3. Blue Letter Bible, s.v. "*sphragizō*," accessed June 17, 2024, https://www.blueletterbible.org/lexicon/g4972/esv/tr/0-1/.

WEEK 2, DAY 2

1. Blue Letter Bible, s.v. "*aiteō*," accessed June 17, 2024, https://www.blueletterbible.org/lexicon/g154/esv/tr/0-1/.

WEEK 2, DAY 3

1. Blue Letter Bible, s.v. "*emphanizō*," accessed June 17, 2024, https://www.blueletterbible.org/lexicon/g1718/esv/mgnt/0-1/.

WEEK 2, DAY 4

1. Blue Letter Bible, s.v. "*yādâ*," accessed June 17, 2024, https://www.blueletterbible.org/lexicon/h3034/esv/wlc/0-1/.

WEEK 2, DAY 5

1. Blue Letter Bible, s.v. "*homothymadon*," accessed June 17, 2024, https://www.blueletterbible.org/lexicon/g3661/esv/mgnt/0-1/.
2. Blue Letter Bible, s.v. "*homothymadon*."

WEEK 3, DAY 1

1. Wiersbe, *The Wiersbe Bible Commentary*, 778.
2. Blue Letter Bible, s.v. "*hyperbolē*," accessed June 17, 2024, https://www.blueletterbible.org/lexicon/g5236/esv/tr/0-1/.

WEEK 3, DAY 2

1. Blue Letter Bible, s.v. "*kainos*," accessed June 17, 2024, https://www.blueletterbible.org/lexicon/g2537/esv/tr/0-1/.
2. *Merriam-Webster*, s.v. "fresh," accessed June 17, 2024, https://www.merriam-webster.com/dictionary/freshness.

WEEK 3, DAY 3

1. "Dwight L. Moody," Goodreads, accessed June 17, 2024, http://www.goodreads.com/quotes/4474-i-firmly-believe-that-the-moment-our-hearts-are-emptied.
2. Blue Letter Bible, s.v. "*poieō*," accessed June 17, 2024, https://www.blueletterbible.org/lexicon/g4160/esv/tr/0-1/.

WEEK 3, DAY 4

1. Blue Letter Bible, s.v. "*pimplēmi*," accessed June 17, 2024, https://www.blueletterbible.org/lexicon/g4130/esv/tr/0-1/.
2. Blue Letter Bible, s.v. "*dynamis*," accessed June 17, 2024, https://www.blueletterbible.org/lexicon/g1411/esv/tr/0-1/.
3. "Billy Sunday," Goodreads, accessed June 17, 2024, https://www.goodreads.com/quotes/190658-the-only-way-to-keep-a-broken-vessel-full-is.

WEEK 4, DAY 2

1. Blue Letter Bible, s.v. "*elpis*," accessed June 17, 2024, https://www.blueletterbible.org/lexicon/g1680/esv/tr/0-1/.
2. "Dwight L. Moody," AZ Quotes, accessed June 17, 2024, https://www.azquotes.com/quote/596116.
3. Blue Letter Bible, s.v. "*oikeō*," accessed June 17, 2024, https://www.blueletterbible.org/lexicon/g3611/esv/tr/0-1/.

WEEK 4, DAY 3

1. "Instrument for Getting God's Will Done on Earth," Family Times, accessed June 17, 2024, https://www.family-times.net/commentary/instrument-for-getting-gods-will-done-on-earth/.
2. "Smith Wigglesworth," AZ Quotes, accessed June 17, 2024, https://www.azquotes.com/quote/1344604.

WEEK 4, DAY 4

1. Blue Letter Bible, s.v. "*haplōs*," accessed June 17, 2024, https://www.blueletterbible.org/lexicon/g574/esv/tr/0-1/.
2. Wiersbe, *The Wiersbe Bible Commentary*, 870.

WEEK 5, DAY 1

1. Blue Letter Bible, s.v. "*sphragizō*."
2. "Leonard Ravenhill," AZ Quotes, accessed June 17, 2024, https://www.azquotes.com/quote/668258.
3. Blue Letter Bible, s.v. "*ginōskō*," accessed June 17, 2024, https://www.blueletterbible.org/lexicon/g1097/esv/tr/0-1/.

WEEK 5, DAY 2

1. Blue Letter Bible, s.v. "*peripateō*," accessed June 17, 2024, https://www.blueletterbible.org/lexicon/g4043/kjv/tr/0-1/.
2. Blue Letter Bible, s.v. "*nāhal*," accessed June 18, 2024, https://www.blueletterbible.org/lexicon/h5095/esv/wlc/0-1/.

WEEK 5, DAY 3

1. *Cambridge Dictionary*, s.v. "whisper," accessed June 17, 2024, https://dictionary.cambridge.org/us/dictionary/english/whisper.
2. Blue Letter Bible, s.v. "*phōnē*," accessed June 17, 2024, https://www.blueletterbible.org/lexicon/g5456/esv/tr/0-1/.
3. Blue Letter Bible, s.v. "*phainō*," accessed June 17, 2024, https://www.blueletterbible.org/lexicon/g5316/esv/tr/0-1/.
4. *Merriam-Webster*, s.v. "fellowship," accessed June 17, 2024, https://www.merriam-webster.com/dictionary/fellowship.
5. "Charles Haddon Spurgeon," Goodreads, accessed June 17, 2024, https://www.goodreads.com/author/quotes/2876959.Charles_Hardon-Spurgeon?page=2.

WEEK 5, DAY 4

1. Blue Letter Bible, s.v. "*dynamis*," accessed June 17, 2024, https://www.blueletterbible.org/lexicon/g1411/esv/tr/0-1/.

WEEK 6, DAY 1

1. Blue Letter Bible, s.v. "*rō'š*," accessed June 17, 2024, https://www.blueletterbible.org/lexicon/h7218/esv/tr/0-1/.

WEEK 6, DAY 2

1. Blue Letter Bible, s.v. "*christos*," accessed June 17, 2024, https://www.blueletterbible.org/lexicon/g5547/esv/tr/0-1/.

WEEK 6, DAY 3

1. Blue Letter Bible, s.v. "*prothesis*," accessed June 17, 2024, https://www.blueletterbible.org/lexicon/g4286/esv/tr/0-1/.

WEEK 6, DAY 4

1. Blue Letter Bible, s.v. "*tarassō*," accessed June 17, 2024, https://www.blueletterbible.org/lexicon/g5015/esv/tr/0-1/.
2. Blue Letter Bible, s.v. "*eirēnē*," accessed June 17, 2024, https://www.blueletterbible.org/lexicon/g1515/esv/tr/0-1/.
3. Blue Letter Bible, s.v. "*brabeuō*," accessed June 17, 2024, https://www.blueletterbible.org/lexicon/g1018/esv/tr/0-1/.

LEADER RESOURCES

LEADING A SMALL GROUP?

Access all video content plus bonus leader resources online at UnlimitedGuide.info

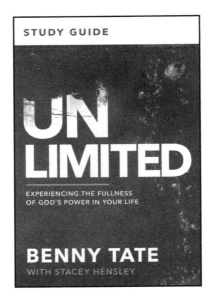